F
Food

Daily Devotions
For Winter

Kenneth E. Hagin

Unless otherwise indicated, all Scripture quotations in this volume are from the *King James Version* of the Bible.

Second Edition
Tenth Printing 1998

ISBN 0-89276-041-9

In the U.S. write:
Kenneth Hagin Ministries
P.O. Box 50126
Tulsa, OK 74150-0126

In Canada write:
Kenneth Hagin Ministries
P.O. Box 335, Station D
Etobicoke (Toronto), Ontario
Canada, M9A 4X3

Preface

Feed your faith daily! It is of utmost importance to your walk with the Lord. I've written these bite-size pieces of "faith food" to aid you in making sure your faith is fed daily.

F. F. Bosworth said, "Most Christians feed their bodies three hot meals a day, their spirits one cold snack a week, and then they wonder why they are so weak in faith."

Say the confessions found on the bottom of each page aloud. Close your eyes and repeat them. They are based on God's Word. When you hear yourself say these confessions, they will register on your spirit. And when God's Word gets down into your spirit, it will control your life!

Kenneth E. Hagin

EL SHADDAI

And when Abram was ninety years old and nine, the Lord appeared to Abram, and said unto him, I AM THE ALMIGHTY GOD; walk before me, and be thou perfect.

— GENESIS 17:1

The original Hebrew of this Old Testament verse reads that God said, "I am El Shaddai."

God was revealed to Israel by seven covenant names, one of which was El Shaddai — which literally means "the God who is more than enough," or, "the All-Sufficient One."

It will help your faith to think of God as "the One who is more than enough!"

Throughout the Old Testament, God revealed Himself as El Shaddai — the God who is more than enough. For example, as God was bringing the children of Israel out of Egyptian bondage, Pharaoh's soldiers went after them to recapture them and make them slaves again. On one side of the children of Israel was the wilderness; on the other side, mountains. The Red Sea lay before them. They seemingly were boxed in, but they looked to God — the God who is more than enough — and He divided the sea! He congealed the depths in the heart of the sea (Exod. 15:8)! He froze the waters! The waters stood up on each side like a wall, and Israel walked across to the other side. Our God is more than enough!

Confession: *My Father is El Shaddai, the God who is more than enough. He's more than any mountain to my right. He's more than any enemy behind me. He's more than any obstacle before me. He is my very own Father. And He is El Shaddai — the God who is more than enough!*

More Than Enough

And the sun stood still, and the moon stayed, until the people had avenged themselves upon their enemies.

— JOSHUA 10:13

We see El Shaddai with Israel in Canaan's land. (And incidently, Canaan is not a type of Heaven. It couldn't be. In Heaven there won't be battles to fight, cities to take, or enemies or giants to overcome — they're here in this world. No, Canaan is a type of the baptism in the Holy Spirit and our rights and privileges in Christ Jesus.) When Israel ran into difficulty in Canaan, Joshua, their leader, spoke to the Lord. *And God stopped the whole universe because a man of God prayed!* God can do that — He's the God who is more than enough!

All through the Old Testament, we see El Shaddai moving in the lives of men and women, prophets, priests, and kings. But He's not just the God of *yesterday*; He's the God of *now*! He didn't identify Himself as "the God who *was* more than enough," or "the God who *will* be more than enough." Too often we relegate everything back in the *past*, saying, "Oh it was wonderful back when God did such things," or to the *future*, saying, "When we all get to Heaven, everything will be wonderful." No, things will be different *here and now* if you will trust in this God who is more than enough!

Confession: I *believe God. I trust in God now. He is more than enough today! He is more than enough to overcome any situation I could face. He is MORE THAN ENOUGH for me.*

HE DELIVERS

Because he hath set his love upon me, therefore will I deliver him . . . . — PSALM 91:14

"I will," or "I shall" is the strongest assertion that can be made in the English language. And in the last part of Psalm 91, there are seven things this God who is more than enough says He will do for the person who has set his love upon Him. (Thank God, I've set my love upon Him — have you?)

Notice that God didn't say, "I *may* do it," or, "If I don't run out of energy, I'll do it. If my power doesn't wane, I'll do it." No! He is the All-Sufficient One, and He said, "I *will* do it."

First, God said, "I will deliver them . . . ." This God who is more than enough is a delivering God. He kept His Word with Abraham, and delivered Israel — and He's still the Deliverer today.

Our God is not the oppressor; He is the Deliverer! Acts 10:38 makes that clear. Satan is the oppressor of mankind — but Jesus is our Deliverer!

Confession: *I have set my love upon God; therefore, He delivers me. He is a delivering God. And God is more than enough. He will never run out of energy. He will never run out of power. God will do all that He has said He will do. He's the All-Sufficient One, and He WILL do it!*

HE ANSWERS

Because he hath set his love upon me, therefore. . . . He shall call upon me, and I will answer him . . . . — PSALM 91:14-15

Call unto me, and I will answer thee, and shew thee great and mighty things, which thou knowest not. — JEREMIAH 33:3

And all things, whatsoever ye shall ask in prayer, believing, ye shall receive. — MATTHEW 21:22

Therefore I say unto you, What things soever ye desire, when ye pray, believe that ye receive them, and ye shall have them. — MARK 11:24

And in that day ye shall ask me nothing. Verily, verily, I say unto you, Whatsoever ye shall ask the Father in my name, he will give it you. Hitherto have ye asked nothing in my name: ask, and ye shall receive, that your joy may be full. — JOHN 16:23-24

These are by no means all of the scriptures on the subject of prayer. But these scriptures alone are enough to set our hearts on fire. They're enough to start us praying. Why? Because El Shaddai said to us, "I will answer." The Almighty God — the One who is more than enough — has promised to answer those who set their love on Him!

Confession: *I have set my love upon Almighty God; therefore, He answers me. I call upon Him, and He answers me. I ask, and He gives me. I seek, and He causes me to find. I knock, and He opens it to me. What things soever I desire, when I pray, I believe that I receive them, and God causes me to have them. Whatever I ask in Jesus' Name, Almighty God gives me. My joy is full!*

He's the Way Out

Because he hath set his love upon me, therefore . . . I will be with him in trouble; I will deliver him . . . . — PSALM 91:14-15

God didn't say you weren't going to have trouble. In fact, He rather infers that you *will* have trouble because you're a Christian! The world will persecute you, talk about you, speak evil of you. An enemy is arrayed against you. The god of this world (2 Cor. 4:4) puts pressure on you at every turn.

Some people think it's God who is putting pressure on them, but it isn't. Jesus contrasted His works and the works of the devil like this: *"The thief cometh not, but for to steal, and to kill, and to destroy: I am come that they might have life, and that they might have it more abundantly"* (John 10:10). God is not a thief. That which steals, and kills, and destroys is the devil — not God.

God says in His Word, *"Many are the afflictions of the righteous: but the Lord delivereth him out of them all"* (Ps. 34:19). The word "afflictions" here means tests and trials. And that's what your troubles are. But the Lord has promised to deliver you out of how many of them: half? No! Out of them *all*! The Lord didn't just promise to be with you in trouble and them stop there. He's there to deliver you out of that trouble. And He's more than enough!

Confession: *I have set my love upon God; therefore, no matter what the test or trial, I know that El Shaddai is with me to deliver me. And He's more than enough!*

He Honors

Because he hath set his love upon me, therefore . . . I will set him on high . . . and honour him. — PSALM 91:14,15

I'd rather have God honor me than to have all the acclaim this world can offer.

The story is told that one day Napoleon was reviewing his troops when his horse began to buck. A young private stepped over, took the horse by the bridle, and quieted him down. Napoleon said, "Thank you, Captain." And the private moved into rank of a captain. But the other officers shunned this young man. They had earned their rank, but his had been granted to him. Napoleon noticed this and called for a full, gala review of his army. He sat this young man on a horse by his side, and they rode out to the parade grounds together. The other officers then began to say, "That fellow's a favorite with Napoleon." And they began to court his favor.

The world may not know it, but the time is coming when they are going to find out that we are favorites with the King of kings and Lord of lords. And they'll wish they had courted our favor. Jesus Himself said, *"To him that overcometh will I grant to sit with me in my throne, even as I also overcame, and am set down with my Father in his throne"* (Rev. 3:21). Jesus' favor far outshines any that this world can bestow.

Confession: *Because I have set my love upon God, He will set me on high. He will honor me. I am a favorite with the King of kings and Lord of lords. I am a favorite with the God who is more than enough!*

LONG LIFE

Because he hath set his love upon me, therefore . . . With long life will I satisfy him . . . . — PSALM 91:14,16

"But, Brother Hagin," somebody said, "I knew a minister who was a wonderful man of God, and he died at age forty-two."

That doesn't mean I have to die young. I don't know what that minister believed — but I know what I believe. And I know that the God Who is more than enough said, "I will satisfy him with long life."

Somebody else will say, "That just means we're going to live forever in Heaven." No, even sinners are going to live forever. They're going to live in one place, and we're going to live in another. That scripture is referring to our enjoying long life here upon this earth.

A reading of Proverbs reveals that the Word of God says that doing certain things will lengthen your life, but doing certain other things will shorten your life. Ephesians 6:1-3 tells children to honor their parents, so *"That it may be well with thee, and thou mayest live long on the earth."* Peter quoted the Psalms assuring us that these promises belong to us (1 Peter 3:10; Ps. 34:12).

Our promised lifespan is seventy or eighty years (Ps. 90:10). But don't compromise. Don't settle for anything less. *And believe God for all you can!*

Confession: *Because I have set my love upon God, El Shaddai will satisfy me with long life. Unless the Lord Jesus Christ returns before I die, I will live out my years in service to God. I will live and work together with God in carrying out His will upon the earth.*

7

SALVATION

Because he hath set his love upon me, therefore . . . [will I] shew him my salvation. — PSALM 91:14,16

Although I cannot agree with all of Dr. C. I. Scofield's notes in his *Reference Bible*, his footnote following Romans 1:16, referring to the word "salvation," is excellent. Dr. Scofield, a Greek and Hebrew scholar, wrote:

> The Greek and Hebrew words for salvation imply the ideas of *deliverance, safety, preservation, healing,* and *soundness* [health].

El Shaddai has promised to show us deliverance . . . safety . . . preservation . . . healing . . . and health. For He has promised to show us His salvation!

Confession: *Because I have set my love upon God, the God who is more than enough has shown me His salvation. He has made known to me the Gospel of Jesus Christ, which is the power of God unto salvation (Rom. 1:16). This Gospel is the power of God unto my deliverance. It is the power of God unto my safety. It is the power of God unto my preservation. It is the power of God unto my healing. It is the power of God unto my health. And it is more than enough!*

CROWNED WITH GLORY

When I view and consider Your heavens, the work of Your fingers, the moon and the stars which You have ordained and established; What is man, that You are mindful of him, and the son of [earthborn] man, that You care for him? Yet You have made him but a little lower than God [or heavenly beings], and You have crowned him with glory and honor. You made him to have dominion over the works of Your hands . . . .
— PSALM 8:3-6 *(Amplified)*

God did not create man for death! Death, sin, sickness, hatred, revenge, and all such tragedies reflect conditions on earth that had no place in the original plan of the Creator. Man was created instead for joy, happiness, and peace!

Man was designed for eternal fellowship with God. He was created in God's very image and likeness (Gen. 1:26,27). He was created for joy, happiness, and peace. And he was created to give God pleasure (Rev. 4:11).

God gave man a place in His creation second only to Himself, with dominion as far reaching as the universe itself (Ps. 8:3-6; Gen. 1:26-28). Adam was the master of himself, of creation, and of Satan. Adam did not have to yield to sin — he had a choice.

Confession: *I will do what I was designed to do; I will fellowship with God. I will give Him pleasure. The Bible says that without faith it is impossible to please God (Heb. 11:6). So I will walk in faith. I will not be dominated by sin, sickness, fear, and doubt, or anything else that is of the devil. I choose to walk with God.*

SHORT OF THE GLORY

For all have sinned, and come short of the glory of God.
— ROMANS 3:23

Man did the *unthinkable*! Given dominion over all the works of God's hand, Adam was originally the god of this world. But Adam *knowingly* committed high treason against God by selling out to Satan the dominion which God had originally given him. Adam's treason was done on such a legal basis that God could not annul the contract He had made with Adam, and which Adam had passed on to Satan. Hence, Satan, not Adam, became the god of this world (2 Cor. 4:4). And thus began Satan's destructive reign.

So spiritual death — which is *separation from God* — came to man. When God came down in the cool of the day to walk and talk with Adam, God called, "Adam, where art thou?" And Adam said, "I hid myself." He was separated from God!

Another aspect of spiritual death — *having Satan's nature* — also came to man. The devil became man's spiritual father. Notice Jesus said to the Pharisees, *"Ye are of your father the devil"* (John 8:44). Man is spiritually a child of the devil. He partakes of his father's nature. This explains why man cannot be saved by conduct. Man cannot stand in the presence of God as he is, having the nature of his father, the devil, in him. If man is ever saved, he must be saved by someone paying the penalty for his sins, and someone giving him a new nature.

Confession: *Thank You, Father, for my new nature. Thank You, Father, that You have made provision for me to be a "partaker of the divine nature" (2 Peter 1:4).*

A Great Plan!

And I will put enmity between thee and the woman, and between thy seed and her seed; it shall bruise thy head, and thou shalt bruise his heel. — GENESIS 3:15

Man fell.

But God had a plan — a great plan — *redemption!* God assumed the liabilities of man's transgressions and redeemed him from Satan's dominion. God had a plan to give *life* back to man. God's plan allowed man's nature to be changed back into harmony with God's nature.

God cannot ignore man's transgressions. Justice demanded that the penalty for man's crime be paid — but man himself was unable to pay it. Therefore, because man couldn't save himself, God had to provide a Redeemer.

No sooner had man fallen under the dominion of his enemy, Satan, than God began to speak forth His plan concerning the Coming One. This One, the seed of woman (for it was prophesied that a woman would give birth to a child independent of natural generation) would break Satan's dominion over man! This One would set men free! This One would bruise the head of the serpent!

In Oriental languages, "bruising the head" means breaking the lordship of a ruler. When God spoke those words to Satan in Genesis 3:15, Satan had just come into the dominion meant to belong to man. But God spoke forth that his Wonderful Seed of woman would come to break Satan's lordship.

Confession: *Thank You, Father, for your great plan of redemption, which You planned and sent the Lord Jesus Christ to consummate.*

IMMANUEL

And he said, Hear ye now, O house of David; Is it a small thing for you to weary men, but will ye weary my God also? Therefore the Lord himself shall give you a sign; Behold, a virgin shall conceive, and bear a son, and shall call his name Immanuel.
— ISAIAH 7:13-14

God began to speak through His prophets, promising that a Redeemer would come who would break Satan's dominion and restore to man his lost dominion.

The prophet Isaiah, for example, looked down through time and pointed to a daughter of David who would give birth to that promised Redeemer 750 years later.

"The Lord Himself will give you a sign," Isaiah prophesied. "He will show you a miracle, a wonder, something out of the ordinary."

What will it be?

A virgin shall conceive, and bear a son. A virgin shall give birth to a son in a supernatural way.

His Name shall be called Immanuel — which means "God with us," or "Incarnation." Here, God suggests the union of deity and humanity.

Confession: *The Lord Himself gave a sign, a wonder. A virgin did conceive and bear a Son. His Name is called Immanuel — God with us. He came to redeem us. Thank You, Father, for your great plan of redemption, which You planned and sent Immanuel to consummate.*

THE SEED

. . . For the Lord hath created a new thing in the earth, A woman shall compass a man. — JEREMIAH 31:22

Adam was created. The rest of the human race was generated by natural processes. If Jesus had been born by natural generation, He would have been a fallen spirit.

But Romans 5:12 tells us, *"Wherefore, as by one man [Adam] sin entered into the world, and death by sin; and so death passed upon all men, for that all have sinned."*

Man is subject to death; to the devil. Thus, man's seed could only produce another fallen man.

Therefore, the Redeemer could not be a subject of death. The Promised Seed had to be One over whom Satan had no legal claims or authority. He had to be brought forth by a special act of divine power. He had to be conceived by the Holy Spirit!

The words God spoke through the prophet Jeremiah could be translated literally as, "A woman shall encompass a man child." The womb of the virgin was simply the receptacle of the Holy Seed until He was brought forth.

Confession: *Thank You, Father, for your great plan of redemption. I am so glad that You created a new thing in the earth. I am so glad that You sent forth the Holy Seed to redeem us.*

From Everlasting

But thou, Bethlehem Ephratah, though thou be little among the thousands of Judah, yet out of thee shall he come forth unto me that is to be ruler in Israel; whose goings forth have been from of old, from everlasting. — MICAH 5:2

This remarkable prophetic utterance about One who would be born of the family of Judah to be a Ruler in Israel states that His goings forth were from old, from everlasting. He has traveled up and down through eternity, and He has left His footprints on the ages!

Too frequently people simply look at the physical side of Jesus' birth and talk about His being born as a little babe — when actually He preexisted with the Father from the beginning!

The Person we now know as Jesus Christ is one of the three Divine Persons of the Deity. As God, He had no beginning.

Confession: *The goings forth of Christ, my Lord, were from of old, from everlasting. As God, He had no beginning. Yet He came forth to this world to redeem me from the dominion of Satan. I can trust this Eternal One with my life.*

FOR MEDITATION

For unto us a child is born, unto us a son is given: and the government shall be upon his shoulder: and his name shall be called Wonderful, Counsellor, The mighty God, The everlasting Father, The Prince of Peace. — ISAIAH 9:6

Divine names and titles ascribed to Jesus prove that He is, by nature, divine and a member of the Godhead:

EMMANUEL (Matt. 1:23) . . . GOD (John 1:1) . . . LORD (Luke 19:34) . . . LORD OF ALL (Acts 10:36) . . . LORD OF GLORY (1 Cor. 2:8) . . . WONDERFUL, COUNSELOR, MIGHTY GOD, EVERLASTING FATHER, PRINCE OF PEACE (Isa. 9:6,7) . . . THE LORD'S CHRIST (Luke 2:26) . . . SON OF GOD (Rom. 1:4) . . . HIS SON (John 3:16-18) . . . MY SON (Matt 3:17) . . . ONLY BEGOTTEN SON (John 1:18) . . . ALPHA AND OMEGA, BEGINNING AND THE END, FIRST AND LAST (Rev. 22:13) . . . THE LORD (Acts 9:17) . . . SON OF THE HIGHEST (Luke 1:32) . . . BREAD OF GOD (John 6:33) . . . HOLY ONE OF GOD (Mark 1:24) . . . THY HOLY CHILD JESUS (Acts 4:30) . . . KING OF KINGS AND LORD OF LORDS (Rev. 19:16) . . . LORD AND SAVIOR (2 Peter 3:2) . . . WORD OF GOD (Rev. 19:13).

Confession: *Jesus is my Lord, My Lord is called Emmanuel, God, Lord of All, Lord of Glory, Wonderful, Counselor, Mighty God, Everlasting Father, Prince of Peace, The Lord's Christ, Son of God, His Son, Only Begotten Son, Alpha and Omega, Beginning and the End, First and Last, The Lord, Son of the Highest, Bread of God, Holy One of God, The Holy Child Jesus, King of kings and Lord of lords, Lord and Savior, Word of God. That's who my Lord is! No wonder Satan cannot dominate me!*

15

For Further Meditation

For it pleased the Father that in him should all fulness dwell.
— COLOSSIANS 1:19

The Word of God plainly teaches that our Redeemer is divine.

These divine offices are ascribed to Him:

CREATOR (Col. 1:16) . . . MEDIATOR (1 Tim. 2:4,5) . . . HEAD OF THE CHURCH . . . (Col. 1: 16-24) . . . SAVIOR (2 Peter 3:2) . . . JUDGE (2 Tim. 4:1) . . . PRESERVER (Heb. 1:1-3) . . . LIFE-GIVER (John 10:28) . . . LORD AND CHRIST (Acts 2:36) . . . RESURRECTION AND LIFE (John 11:25).

Divine character is ascribed to Christ. Ordinary men are sinners by nature, but Christ Jesus is not an ordinary man. He is:

HOLY BY BIRTH (Luke 1:35) . . . RIGHTEOUS (Isa. 53:11) . . . FAITHFUL (Isa 11:5) . . . TRUTH (John 14:6) . . . JUST (John 5:30) . . . GUILELESS (1 Peter 2:22) . . . SINLESS (2 Cor. 5:21) . . . SPOTLESS (1 Peter 1:19) . . . INNOCENT (Matt. 27:4) . . . HARMLESS (Heb. 7:26) . . . OBEDIENT TO EARTHLY PARENTS (Luke 2:51) . . . ZEALOUS (John 2:17) . . . MEEK (Matt. 11:29) . . . LOWLY IN HEART (Matt. 11:29) . . . MERCIFUL (Heb. 2:17) . . . PATIENT (Isa. 53:7) . . . LONG SUFFERING (1 Tim. 1:16) . . . COMPASSIONATE (Matt. 15:32) . . . BENEVOLENT (Acts 10:38) . . . LOVING (John 15:13) . . . SELF-DENYING (2 Cor. 8:9) . . . HUMBLE (Phil. 2:5-11) . . . RESIGNED (Luke 22:42) . . . FORGIVING (Luke 23:34).

Confession: *Jesus Christ is worthy. Thank God for this Worthy One. Thank God for this Divine One. Thank God that One who is the Creator would come to earth from glory to be the Mediator, the Head of the Church, the Savior, the Judge, the Preserver, the Life-Giver, the Lord and Savior. And thank God, this Worthy One is my Lord.*

HUMILITY

Who, being in the form of God, thought it not robbery to be equal with God: But made himself of no reputation, and took upon him the form of a servant, and was made in the likeness of men: And being found in fashion as a man, he humbled himself, and became obedient unto death, even the death of the cross.
— **PHILIPPIANS 2:6-8**

Christ has always existed in the form of God. But He emptied Himself and took the form of a bond servant, being made in the likeness of men.

This suggests a distinct operation of God totally different from natural generation: A miracle. First, God took Christ from the Godhead of Heaven — and then He placed Christ in the womb of a virgin to be united with flesh in a unique conception.

Wherefore when he cometh into the world, he saith, Sacrifice and offering thou wouldest not, but a body hast thou prepared me. — **HEBREWS 10:5**

God prepared a body — a special body — for this Being called the Son of God. In the Incarnation, Christ became a man!

Confession: *Thank You, Jesus, for emptying Yourself and being made in the likeness of men. It was our only hope. Thank You for humbling Yourself and becoming obedient unto death; yes, even the death of the cross. And thank You, Father, for highly exalting Him, and for giving to Him the Name which is above every name. At that Name my knee does bow, and my tongue does confess that Jesus Christ is Lord, to the glory of God the Father (Phil. 2: 9,10).*

INCARNATION

In the beginning was the Word, and the Word was with God, and the Word was God . . . And the Word was made flesh, and dwelt among us, (and we beheld his glory, the glory as of the only begotten of the Father,) full of grace and truth.

— JOHN 1:1,14

Webster defines Incarnation as "The union of divinity with humanity in Jesus Christ."

Incarnation was the only solution to the human problem — the only hope for mankind to be reunited with God. *Any religion that denies the incarnation of Jesus of Nazareth is false!*

This Eternal Being, called Emmanuel — God with us, or Jesus the Christ — is here called the Word. The Word existed in the beginning. The Word was with God — with God in fellowship, in purpose, working with Him. God made the worlds through the Word (Heb. 1:2; John 1:3).

And this Eternal Being was God! He possessed the same nature. He existed in the same form and on an equality with God (Phil. 2:6).

And this Being became flesh! The Word became a man and dwelt among us. He became human — as much a man as if He'd never been anything else, yet He did not cease to be what He had been. The Word made His home among us, and we beheld the glory of God (Col. 1:15; Heb. 1:3).

Confession: *Jesus came and dwelled in flesh so that I might be eternally reunited with the Father. Jesus became like me, so that I could become like Him. I will walk in the reality of what the Incarnation made possible for me. I am reunited with my Father!*

MEDIATOR

For there is one God, and one mediator between God and men, the man Christ Jesus. —1 TIMOTHY 2:5

Man's condition demanded an Incarnation — man had become spiritually dead with no approach to God. The Incarnation of Deity with humanity provided One who could stand as man's Mediator. Equal with God on one hand and united with man on the other, this One could assume the obligations of man's treason and satisfy the claims of Justice, thereby bridging the chasm between God and man.

God created man in His own image, just a little lower than Himself; so nearly like God that it was possible for God and man to become united for eternity in one individual! (When Christ became a man and took on a physical body in the Incarnation, He did so for eternity. Therefore, there is a God-man in Heaven today at the Father's right hand as a result of the Incarnation.) *It was possible for God and man to become united!*

God can dwell in these human bodies of ours, God can impart His *life* and *nature* to our spirits. That's what takes place at the New Birth: Spiritual death is eradicated from the spirit, and God gives man His *life*!

Confession: *Today at the right hand of the Father there is a God-man, our Mediator, Jesus Christ. Jesus bridged the gap for me. He made it possible for spiritual death to depart from my spirit, and for God's own life and nature to take its place in my spirit. Therefore, God now dwells in my spirit. God lives in me!*

HE CAME TO SAVE

And she shall bring forth a son, and thou shalt call his name Jesus: for he shall save his people from their sins.
— MATTHEW 1:21

The first step in redemption was Christ's identification with our humanity. This took place in His Incarnation. Christ was made flesh (John 1:14). Hebrews 2:14 says, *"Forasmuch then as the children are partakers of flesh and blood, he also himself likewise took part of the same . . . ."*

But at the time of His Incarnation, Jesus did not partake of the *nature* that reigned in the spirit of man. Had He done so then, He would have been *spiritually dead* during His earthly ministry! Then He could not have pleased the Father by doing His own will. No, His identification with the Spirit nature of man didn't take place until His crucifixion.

There God actually made Jesus Christ to become sin for us (2 Cor. 5:21). Our sin nature itself was laid upon Jesus Christ until He became all that spiritual death had made man. In the mind of God, it was not Jesus Christ who hung on the cross; it was the human race who hung there. Therefore, each of us may say with Paul, "I was crucified with Christ."

Confession: *Because Jesus came to save me from my sins, I can claim Galatians 2:20, "I am crucified with Christ: nevertheless I live; yet not I, but Christ liveth in me: and the life which I now live in the flesh I live by the faith of the Son of God, who loved me, and gave himself for me."*

THAT WE MIGHT BE SONS

But when the fulness of the time was come, God sent forth his Son, made of a woman, made under the law, To redeem them that were under the law, that we might receive the adoption of sons. And because ye are sons, God hath sent forth the Spirit of his Son into your hearts, crying, Abba, Father. Wherefore thou art no more a servant, but a son; and if a son, then an heir of God through Christ. — GALATIANS 4:4-7

The object of the Incarnation was that man might be given the right to become a child of God (John 1:12).

Man could become a child of God only by receiving the nature of God; therefore, Christ came that man might receive eternal life (John 10:10; 1 John 5:11,12).

And man could receive eternal life only after he had been legally redeemed from Satan's authority (Col. 1:13,14).

Confession: *God sent forth His Son to redeem us, that we might become sons of God. I have received Christ; therefore, I have life. I am a son of God. And because I am, God has sent forth the Spirit of His Son into my heart, crying, "Abba, Father." I am no more a servant; but a son. I am an heir of God through Christ.*

HE CAME TO DECLARE HIM

No man hath seen God at any time; the only begotten Son, which is in the bosom of the Father, he hath declared him.
— JOHN 1:18

How Jesus realized and appreciated the phase of His mission on earth which had to do with declaring the true nature of His Father!

A noted Bible scholar once said, concerning the Incarnation, "We know now that God is like this that we have seen in Jesus. He is Christ-like. And if He is, He is a good God and trustable. If the heart that is in back of the universe is like this gentle heart without qualifications and without reservations. I know nothing higher to say of God than that He should live like Christ . . . . Strange, a man lived among us and when we think of God we think of Him in terms of this man or He is not good. We may transfer every single moral quality in Jesus to God without loss or degradation to our thought of God. On the contrary, by thinking of Him in terms of Jesus we heighten our views of God. All those who have tried to think of Him in other terms have lowered and impoverished our idea of Him."

Confession: *Jesus has declared God the Father to me. I know what God is like — He's like Jesus! God is a good God — and I do trust Him.*

INCARNATE REVELATOR

Jesus saith unto him [Philip] *. . . he that hath seen me hath seen the Father . . . .* — JOHN 14:9

Man born into a world ruled by Satan did not by nature know his Creator. Since Adam's sin — when man died *spiritually* — God and man had been spiritually separated.

Man desperately needed an Incarnation. The incarnation of Jesus Christ — God manifested in the flesh — gave to the world the true knowledge of the nature of God.

Spiritually dead men couldn't know the nature of the Creator without a revelation from Him. God had been conceived as weird, cruel, grotesque, immoral, aloof, or, perhaps, an impersonal energy, but He was never thought of as a God of love — a loving Heavenly Father.

"What's he *really* like?" people will inquire about some movie star, TV personality, politician, etc. And sometimes those close to that celebrity will attempt in an interview to tell what he is really like.

"What's God *really* like?" people want to know.

Friends, if you want to know what God is really like — *just look at Jesus!*

Confession: *I have seen Jesus in the revelation of God's Word. Therefore, I have seen the Father. I know what the Father is like. He's just like Jesus! He's a God of love. He's a Father God. And because of Jesus, He's my very own Father. I am His very own child. I'm so thankful for this great plan of redemption which included revealing my Father to the world.*

HIS GLORY

And the Word became flesh. And pitched his tent among us. And we gazed upon his glory — a glory . . . Full of favour and truth.
— JOHN 1:14 (*Rotherham*)

I love Rotherham's translation of John 1:14 — it is so beautiful.

We've tended to think of Christ's coming to the earth as a man only in terms of His self-denial in leaving glory, or else in terms of His suffering on this earth. But I believe it was a joy to Christ, who so loved man and so desired man's fellowship, to "pitch His tent" among us so that He might give to alienated man — who had never known his Creator — a true conception of His Heavenly Father.

It was *good tidings of great joy* which the angel proclaimed to the shepherds — and to all people everywhere. Man, separated from God for four thousand years, could not gaze upon God's glory, could not see God, could now know God as He is, and could now be reunited with Him!

And the angel said unto them, Fear not: for, behold, I bring you good tidings of great joy, which shall be to all people. For unto you is born this day in the city of David a Saviour, which is Christ the Lord. — LUKE 2:10-11

The Word has become flesh!

Confession: *Like the multitude of the heavenly host, I, too, am praising God. Praise God for sending GOOD TIDINGS of GREAT JOY! Praise God for sending a SAVIOR! Praise God for CHRIST THE Lord! Praise God for allowing us to gaze upon HIS GLORY!*

LOVE SENT HIS SON TO SAVE

. . . For that which is conceived in her
is of the Holy Ghost.
And she shall bring forth a son,
and thou shalt call his name JESUS:
for he shall save his people from their sins.

For God so loved the world,
that he gave his only begotten Son,
that whosoever believeth in him
should not perish,
but have everlasting life.

For God sent not his Son into the world
to condemn the world;
but that the world through him
might be saved.

— **MATTHEW 1:20,21; JOHN 3:16,17**

Our Father

. . . For your Father knoweth what things ye have need of, before ye ask him. After this manner therefore pray ye: Our Father . . . .
— MATTHEW 6:8,9

Even Israel, to whom God had given as clear revelation of Himself as it was possible to give spiritually dead men, did not really know God. They didn't recognize *God manifested in the flesh* when Jesus stood in their midst. (Under the Old Covenant, God's Presence was shut up in the Holy of Holies.)

Thus, it was into a hard, harsh atmosphere of Justice that Jesus Christ came. And the Jews of His day could not understand Him. He talked about God as His *Father.* He told of the Father's *love* and *care* for His own! It mystified them. When Jesus introduced God as a Father God of love, His words, for the most part, fell upon unresponsive ears.

Yet we must admit, as we meditate on Jesus' words about the love of God, that even born-again children of God sometimes fail to see God's love side. Israel never grasped it. They didn't understand who it was Jesus was talking about. It was new to them. To tell the truth, it's new to most church members today! They have been taught to fear God, and to shrink from a God of Justice. They've never really seen the love side of God that Jesus came to reveal.

Confession: *I hereby make a quality decision to see and know the love side of God that Jesus came to reveal. I will mediate on Jesus' revelation of God until I really know Him as my Father God of love.*

A FATHER'S PART

Therefore take no thought, saying, What shall we eat? or, What shall we drink? or, Wherewithal shall we be clothed? (For after all these things do the Gentiles seek:) for your heavenly Father knoweth that ye have need of all these things. But seek ye first the Kingdom of God, and his righteousness; and all these things shall be ADDED unto you. Take therefore no thought for the morrow: for the morrow shall take thought for the things of itself. Sufficient unto the day is the evil thereof.

— MATTHEW 6:31-34

Added to you! Not taken away! That proves that the Father cares for His own.

Another translation reads, "Be not therefore anxious for the morrow." You see, God doesn't want His children to be anxious or to worry. What God is saying here is, "Have no worry, no fret, no anxiety. Because I am your Heavenly Father, I know you have need of these things. But seek first the Kingdom of God and His righteousness, and all these things shall be added unto you."

That's what God our Father is saying! If God is your Father, you may be assured that He will take a father's place and perform a father's part. You may be certain that if God is your Father, He loves you, and He will care for you. Praise God, I'm glad He's my Father! Is He yours?

Confession: *I do not worry about what I shall eat or drink or what I shall wear. My Heavenly Father knows I have need of all these things. I have sought first the Kingdom of God and His righteousness, and all these things are added unto me.*

THE FATHER'S LOVE

He that hath my commandments, and keepeth them, he it is that loveth me: and he that loveth me shall be loved of my Father, and I will love him, and will manifest myself to him. Judas saith unto him, not Iscariot, Lord, how is it that thou wilt manifest thyself unto us, and not unto the world? Jesus answered and said unto him, If a man love me, he will keep my words: and my Father will love him, and we will come unto him, and make our abode with him. — JOHN 14:21-23

Two things are emphasized in today's text:

1. *"He that hath my commandments, and keepeth them . . . ,"* Jesus said. Keep in mind what Jesus' commandments are. Jesus said, *"A new commandment I give unto you, That ye love one another; as I have loved you . . ."* (John 13:34). There's no reason for you to worry about any other commandments. Walking in love sums up the whole business, because the Word of God says, *". . . Love is the fulfilling of the law"* (Rom. 13:10). (If you keep Jesus' commandments, you will have fulfilled the rest of the commandments.)

2. *". . . Shall be loved of my Father . . . ."* If you walk in love, you are walking in God's realm, because God is love. God's very nature, because He is love, compels Him to care for us, protect us, and shield us!

Confession: *I have Jesus' commandments, and I keep them. I love others as God has loved me. I walk in love toward my brethren. I show my love for Jesus by keeping His love commandment. I am loved of the Father!*

HOW MUCH MORE

If ye then, being evil, know how to give good gifts unto your children, how much more shall your Father which is in heaven give good things to them that ask him? — MATTHEW 7:11

Would you, as a parent, plan, purpose, and will for your children to go through life poverty-stricken, sick, downtrodden, downcast, down-and-out, their nose to the grindstone? No! Assuredly not!

My younger brother had a difficult time getting his education. Our father left when this brother was six months old. He graduated from high school during the Depression by working the 11 p.m. to 7 a.m. shift at a local cotton mill and then going to school immediately after getting off work.

In time, this brother married, had a son, and became a very successful businessman. He said to me — and I guess this has been a driving force in my brother's life — "I'd rather let my boy die now than to have it like I had it. But I'm going to see to it that he doesn't have it rough like I did."

My brother worked hard to provide a better life for his family than he had known growing up. Just looking at it from the natural standpoint, he did all this because he loved them. And that's what Jesus meant when He said that if natural men know how to give good gifts to their children, *how much more* will our loving Heavenly Father give good things to those who ask Him!

Confession: *Even good natural fathers know how to give good gifts to their children. HOW MUCH MORE will my Father in Heaven give good things to me when I ask Him?*

HUSBANDMAN

I am the true vine, and my Father is the husbandman.
— JOHN 15:1

My Heavenly Father is the Caretaker.
He is he Protector.
He is the Shield.
He is the Sustainer.
He is the Trainer.
He is the Educator.
The Greek word translated "husbandman" involves all those shades of meaning. As the husbandman trains the branches of a vine, so God trains the branches of the Body of Christ.
And remember, God is love!

Confession: *Jesus is the true vine. I am a branch. My Father is the husbandman. He is my Caretaker, my Protector, my Shield, my Sustainer, my Trainer, my Educator. I will bear much fruit!*

LOVER

For the Father himself loveth you, because ye have loved me, and have believed that I came out from God. — JOHN 16:27

Nothing can be stronger or more comforting than the fact that the Father Himself knows you, loves you, and longs to bless you!

In fact, John 17:23 says that *God loves us as He loved Jesus.* What a staggering thought! Yet it is true! Jesus said it!

God the Father is *your* Father! He cares for you. He is interested in you individually — not just as a group, or a body of believers, or a church. God is interested in each of His children, and He loves each one of us with the same love.

Get acquainted with your Father through His Word. It is in His Word that you will learn about your Heavenly Father, about His love, His nature, how He cares for you, how He loves you. He is everything the Word says He is. And He will do everything the Word says He will do!

Confession: *I love Jesus, and I believe He came out from God. Therefore, the Father Himself loves me. God knows me. He cares for me. He longs to bless me. He is interested in my well-being. I get acquainted with Him through the Word. God is everything the Word says He is. He will do everything the Word says He will do.*

RESOLVED: TO GROW

Fight the good fight of faith . . . . — 1 TIMOTHY 6:12

The only fight the Christian is called upon to fight is the *faith fight*.

If you're in any other kind of fight, you're in the wrong fight! There's no need to fight the devil — Jesus has already defeated him. There's no need fighting sin — Jesus is the cure for sin. But there is a fight (and therefore enemies, or hindrances) to faith.

The greatest enemy to faith is lack of understanding of God's Word. In fact, all hindrances to faith center around this lack of knowledge, because you cannot believe or have faith beyond your actual knowledge of the Word of God.

However, your *faith* will automatically grow as your *understanding* of God's Word grows (Rom. 10:17). If your faith is not growing, it's because your knowledge of God's Word is not growing. And you cannot grow or develop spiritually if you are not growing in faith.

The best resolution you can make today is that in the upcoming year, your knowledge of God's Word will grow. Then give yourself to the study of God's Word! It will automatically follow that your faith will grow. Hence, you will grow and develop spiritually.

Confession: *In the upcoming year, my faith will grow. I am determined that my knowledge of God's Word will grow. My understanding of God's Word will grow. Therefore, faith will come. My faith will grow. I will grow and develop spiritually this year!*

FAITH FOLLOWS LIGHT

The entrance of thy words giveth light . . . .
— PSALM 119:130

As a teenager, I became bedfast. Medical science said I would die. Now, I'd heard the New Birth preached all my life. I knew what God's will was concerning salvation. And when I came to the Lord while bedfast, I had no doubt that He would hear me. I had no lack of understanding along that line. Therefore, I had no doubt or unbelief concerning salvation. I received salvation, and I knew that I was saved.

But — I was still bedfast! I certainly had a lack of understanding of God's Word concerning divine healing, prayer, and faith. About all I had ever heard was preachers say, "Just leave it to the Lord. He knows best." (Yes, but in His Word, God has made provision for us to *have* His best!)

In time, after much study of the Bible, I saw the exact steps I needed to take in prayer, and I saw just how to release my faith. Had I known these things earlier, I could have been off that bed months before I was. God didn't have a certain "set time" to heal me. No! He's the same every day! The trouble was on my end of the line. As soon as I found out what God's Word said about healing and acted upon it, I got results! As soon as light comes, faith is there.

Confession: *I will find out what God's Word says, and I will act on it. I will get results. I will see to it that God's Word finds entrance into my spirit. Light will come — and faith will follow.*

33

KNOW YOU'RE NEW

Therefore if any man be in Christ, he is a new creature: old things are passed away; behold, all things are become new.
— 2 CORINTHIANS 5:17

Today's text is one of my favorite scriptures. I got ahold of it while I was still a bedfast teenager. And when I came off that bed healed, I told everyone I met, "I'm a new creature!"

Meditate on this verse today, because if you do not understand the truth of what the New Birth is, it will hinder your faith and will keep you from receiving the blessings God intends you to have.

The spiritual nature of man, you see, is a fallen nature — a satanic nature. Man got the satanic nature from Satan when Adam sinned. And no man can change his own human nature. *But God can!*

When you were born again, something went on *inside* you — instantaneously! That old satanic nature went out of you. And the very life and nature of God came into you! God created you as a brand-new creature — a new creation. The man on the inside — *the real you, which is a spirit man* — *has already become a new man in Christ.*

So don't look at yourself from the physical, from the outside, from natural. Look at yourself from the spiritual standpoint. See yourself as a new creature in Christ. That's how God sees you!

Confession: *I am a new creature. Old things inside me passed away. All things inside me became new. I have a new life. I have a new nature. I have the life of God!*

SAY YOU'RE NEW

I am crucified with Christ: nevertheless I live; yet not I, but Christ liveth in me: and the life which I now live in the flesh I live by the faith of the Son of God, who loved me, and gave himself for me.
— GALATIANS 2:20

I was healed on a Tuesday. That Saturday I walked to town, and I happened to run into a friend of mine. We had been bosom buddies. But during the sixteen months I had been bedfast, he had seen me only once.

He was the same old creature he had always been — but I had become a new creature. He laughed about the things we used to do. Pointing to a building down the street, he said, "Remember the night . . ." and he went on to talk about the time I had picked the lock on the door so some boys could go in and steal candy. I sat there with a mask-like look on my face, as if I didn't know what he was talking about. (I remembered it well enough, but I wanted to use this as an opportunity to witness to him.)

"What's the matter with you? You act like you don't remember — and you were the ringleader," he finally said.

"Lefty, the fellow you were with that night is dead."

"You're not dead! I know you almost died, but you're not dead! That's you sitting there!"

"Oh," I said, "you're looking at the house I live in — my body. The man on the inside who gave permission to the body to pick that lock, is gone. And this man on the inside is now a new creature in Christ Jesus."

Confession: *I am a new creature in Christ Jesus. I hold fast to the confession that I am a new creature.*

Brand New Man

As newborn babes, desire the sincere milk of the word, that ye may grow thereby. — 1 PETER 2:2

When the sinner come to Jesus, his sins are remitted — blotted out. But not only are his sins blotted out — but all that he was, spiritually speaking, in the sight of God — is blotted out. His sins cease to exist. He becomes a new man in Christ Jesus. *God does not seen anything in that person's life before the moment he was born again!*

In today's text, Peter is writing to born-again Christians who have become new men in Christ. The Bible, you see, teaches a similarity between physical growth and spiritual growth. No one is born as a full-grown human being; we are born as babies in the natural, and then we grow up. Likewise, no one is born as a full-grown Christian. Christians are born as spiritual babies, and they grow up. Look at a newborn babe in the natural lying in its mother's arms, its outstanding characteristic is innocence. People say to the baby, "You sweet little innocent thing." No one thinks of that baby as having a past! So do you see what God is saying here through Peter? God is saying to people who have been born again and are now babes in Christ, "As *newborn babes . . . .*" In other words, God is saying, "You have become a new creature — a newborn babe! Your past is gone! I'm not remembering anything against you!"

Confession: *I am a brand-new creature. I'm a brand-new man [or woman]. All that I was before I was born into the family of God is blotted out. I'm God's child — His babe — His very own child.*

NO MORE

This is the covenant that I will make with them after those days, saith the Lord, I will put my laws into their hearts, and in their minds will I write them; And their sins and iniquities will I remember no more. — HEBREWS 10:16,17

When God looks at you, He doesn't remember that you have any past — so why should you remember it? It can hinder your faith.

In talking with people, many have told me, "Brother Hagin, before I was ever saved, I lived such an awful life." then they have told me they don't believe the Lord will do anything for them, such as heal them, or answer their prayers, because they lived such sinful lives before they were saved. They have a complete lack of understanding concerning the New Birth, and concerning the new creature they have become.

When the sinner comes to Christ, he receives *remission* — a blotting out — of sins.

And after a person is a Christian, he can receive *forgiveness* of sins that he may commit: *"If we confess our sins, he is faithful and just to forgive us our sins, and to cleanse us from all unrighteousness"* (1 John 1:9). How long do you think it takes God to forgive us? Ten minutes? Ten years? No, God instantly forgives us! And He instantly cleanses us when we come to Him according to this scripture.

Confession: *My Father does not remember my sins and iniquities. Neither do I remember them. I stand in God's presence as if I had never sinned.*

INSIDE-OUT

But I keep under my body, and bring it into subjection: lest that by any means, when I have preached to others, I myself should be a castaway. — 1 CORINTHIANS 9:27

As a Christian, learn to let the new man in the inside dominate your outward man. The outward man is not a new man. The body has not been born again. The body will keep on wanting to do the things it has always done — things that are wrong. Paul's body did! This great apostle wouldn't have had to keep his body under if it were not wanting to do things which were wrong. So don't be surprised when your body wants to do wrong things.

We have the flesh to contend with in this world. The devil works through the flesh. Because we experience trials and temptations in the flesh, the devil tells Christians, "You must not even be saved! If you were saved, you wouldn't want to do that." Satan will insinuate it's "you" who wants to do wrong, when really "you" the man on the inside — the new man — *doesn't* want to do wrong.

Do you need to break a habit? Conquer an old temptation? Walk in victory over the flesh? Do what Paul did. Say what Paul said. Paul said, "I don't let my body rule me." Who is "I"? "I" is the man on the inside. Paul called his body "it," and he called himself, the man on the inside, "I." Paul said, "I keep under my body, and bring *it* into subjection . . . ." Into subjection to what? To the inward man!

Confession: *I keep my body under. I don't let my body rule me. "I" bring my body into subjection to "me."*

MERE MEN? NO!

And I, brethren, could not speak unto you as unto spiritual, but as unto carnal, even as unto babes in Christ. . . .For ye are yet carnal: for whereas there is among you envying, and strife, and divisions, are ye not carnal, and walk as men?

— 1 CORINTHIANS 3:3

With most Christians, I'm sorry to say, the inward man does not rule the outward man. Instead, the body rules the inward man — and that's what makes carnal Christians. One translation of our text says "body-ruled" instead of "carnal." And that's what carnal Christians are — body ruled.

"Ye are yet carnal . . . And walk as men," Paul told the Corinthians. In other words, they were living like people who had never been born again. I like the way *The Amplified Bible* translates verse three: ". . . For as long as [there are] envying and jealously and wrangling and factions among you, are you not unspiritual and of the flesh, behaving yourselves after a human standard and like mere (unchanged) men?"

Don't do it! Refuse to live like mere men! Live like the new creature you are! Determine to let the new man in Christ — with all that is in him — dominate your being.

Confession: *I refuse to walk as a mere man. I am changed. I am a new creature in Christ. I will grow up in Christ. I will grow up spiritually. "I" — the man on the inside — will dominate my being. I will walk as a spiritual man. I will behave myself after the standard of God's Word. I will walk in love. I will walk in faith!*

SPIRITUAL SERVICE

I beseech you therefore, brethren, by the mercies of God, that ye present your bodies a living sacrifice, holy, acceptable unto God, which is your reasonable service. — ROMANS 12:1

"You" are to do something with your body. For if you don't, nothing will ever be done with it "You," the inward man, have become a new man in Christ. "You" have received eternal life. When eternal life — which is the life and nature of God — is imparted to your spirit, it changes "you."

You won't have any trouble with "you," but you will have trouble with the flesh. People say, "You have to die out to old *self*." No, you don't. That old self is dead, and you have a new self in the place of him. But what you need to die out to is the *flesh.*

Isn't the flesh the old self? No, it isn't. Your flesh is the outward man, the body. And it's the same old flesh it was *before* you were saved!

Your body is the house you live in, and "you" — not God — are the caretaker of that house. "You" do something with your body. You are to present it to God as *". . . a living sacrifice, holy, acceptable unto God . . . ."* Another translation concludes this verse with the phrase *". . . which is your spiritual service."*

Confession: *I am a new creature in Christ. I hold fast to this confession. And the new man on the inside of me is being manifested on the outside and through the flesh. I dominate my body. I present it to God, as a living sacrifice, holy, acceptable to Him, which is my spiritual service.*

IN HIM

Blessed be the God and Father of our Lord Jesus Christ, who hath blessed us with all spiritual blessings in heavenly places in Christ.
— EPHESIANS 1:3

From the day that you were born again until the day you step off into eternity, God has already made provision for you in Christ Jesus. Everything you need, "He *hath* blessed" you with. In the mind of God, it is yours!

People often ask me how to study the Bible. Although I have many suggestions, here is the one I present everywhere I go. As a believer, a Christian, follow this method as you go through the New Testament; primarily the Epistles. (I encourage you to spend most of your time in the Epistles, because they are the letters written to you, the believer. Study the Old Testament, too, but don't spend most of your time there. Spend most of your time in the New Testament. Why? Because we're not living under the Old Covenant; we're living under the New Covenant.) In these Epistles, which are written to the Church, find and underline all expressions such as "in Christ," "by Christ," "in whom," "in Him," and so forth. Write them down. Meditate on them. Begin to confess them with your mouth. As far as God is concerned, everything you have, or are, in Christ, is already so. God has already done it all in Christ. However, it is your believing and your confessing that will make it real to you.

Confession: *I am a new creature IN CHRIST. God the Father HAS blessed me with all spiritual blessings in heavenly places IN CHRIST.*

HEART AND MOUTH

For with the heart man believeth unto righteousness; and with the mouth confession is made unto salvation.

— ROMANS 10:10

It is always with the *heart* that man believes — and with the *mouth* that confession is "made unto." When you *believe* something with your heart and *confess* it with your mouth, then it becomes real to you. *Faith's confessions create realities!*

For example, Hebrews 9:12 says, *"Neither by the blood of goats and calves, but by his own blood he entered in ONCE into the holy place, having obtained eternal redemption for us."* Jesus will never have to do that again; He has already done it once and for all time. And Romans 10:10 tells us how we obtain the reality of that salvation: By *believing* with the heart — the inner man — and *confessing* with the mouth.

As you read some of the "in Christ," "in Him," "in whom" scriptures, it may not seem like you really have what these scriptures say you have. But if you will begin to *confess* (because you do *believe* God's Word in your heart), This is mine. This is who I am. This is what I have." Then it will become real to you. It is already real in the spirit realm. But you want it to become real in this physical realm where you are living.

Confession: *With my heart I believe God's Word. And with my mouth I make confession of its promises and provisions. My faith confessions create the reality of those promises and provisions in my life. I am who God says I am. Now! I have what God says I have. Now!*

WE WERE HEALED!

Who his own self bare our sins in his own body on the tree, that we, being dead to sins, should live unto righteousness: by whose stripes ye were healed. — 1 PETER 2:24

Years ago, a woman was carried into the service. She had not walked in four years, and doctors said she would never walk again. I sat down beside her and placed my open Bible on her lap.

"Sister, please read that verse out loud," I said.

She read First Peter 2:24 aloud. And when she ended with *". . . by whose stripes ye were healed,"* I asked, "Is 'were' past tense, present tense, or future tense?":

I will never forget her reaction, *"Were* is past tense," she exclaimed. "And if we *were* healed, then I *was!*" She accepted God's Word with the enthusiasm and simplicity of a child — the way we must.

And that's how God records it in His Word. He doesn't promise to heal us, because He's already provided healing for us almost 2,000 years ago! Healing is something we already have *in Christ*.

This woman's face lit up as she lifted her hands and said, "Praise God! Lord, I'm so glad I'm healed! Lord, I'm so glad I can walk again! (And she hadn't walked a step yet.) I'm so glad I'm not helpless anymore. I'm so glad I can wait on myself . . ."

"Rise and walk!" I said. The woman leaped to her feet!

Confession: *By His stripes we WERE healed. If we were, then I was. I AM healed. Healing is mine. I have it now!*

REDEEMED FROM THE CURSE

. . . These curses shall come upon thee, and overtake thee . . . If thou wilt not observe to do all the words of this law . . . Also every sickness, and every plague, which is not written in the book of this law . . . . — DEUTERONOMY 28:15,58;61

Christ hath redeemed us from the curse of the law, being made a curse for us: for it is written, Cursed is every one that hangeth on a tree. — GALATIANS 3:13

The Bible says that all sickness and disease is a curse of the law. In Deuteronomy 28, the law specifically named eleven diseases as being a curse of the law; then verse sixty-one encompasses all sicknesses and disease as a curse of the law.

But Christ has redeemed us from the curse of the law! Christ is not going to redeem us; He *has already* redeemed us.

Peter, looking back to the sacrifice at Calvary, said, *". . . by whose stripes ye were healed."* Not *going to be*, but *were!*

God remembers that He laid on Jesus not only the sins and iniquities of us all, but also our sicknesses and diseases (Isa. 53:4,5). Jesus remembers that He bore our sins and sicknesses for us (Matt. 8:17). Therefore, the Holy Spirit inspired Peter to write, *". . . by whose stripes ye were healed."*

Confession: *According to Deuteronomy 28, all sickness and disease is a curse of the law. But according to Galatians 3:13, Christ has redeemed me from the curse of the law. Therefore, I am redeemed from sickness!*

RECONCILED

It was God [personally present] in Christ, reconciling and restoring the world to favor with Himself, not counting up and holding against [men] their trespasses [but cancelling them]; and committing to us the message of reconciliation — (of the restoration to favor). — 2 CORINTHIANS 5:19 *(Amplified)*

"Brother Hagin," a woman asked, "why don't I get healed? I know God has promised to heal me."

I understood her problem and tried to help her. "No ma'am, God hasn't promised to heal you any more than He has promised to save the lost. Nowhere in God's Word does it say, 'God has promised to save you.' No, God's Word declares that God has already done something about your salvation. God laid your sins and iniquities on Jesus."

God *has already* reconciled us to Himself by Christ. And He gave *us* the ministry of reconciliation. We are to tell people that God was personally present with Jesus Christ reconciling the world to favor with Himself. God is not imputing (counting up) or holding against men their trespasses anymore.

"Well," someone said, "we'll all be saved then, won't we?" No, people must *accept* that reconciliation God offers. We are, by nature, children of the devil, therefore, must be born again!

Confession: *I am reconciled to God by Christ. I am restored to favor with God. And God has given me the ministry of reconciliation.*

MIGHTY WEAPON

For the weapons of our warfare are not carnal, but mighty through God to the pulling down of strong holds.
— 2 CORINTHIANS 10:4

Although we have been made new creatures — although we are created by God in Christ Jesus; and although we are transferred out from under Satan's authority — we still live in a world ruled by Satan.

The Bible calls Satan "the god of this world" (2 Cor. 4:4). Satan is also called "the prince of the power of the air" (Eph. 2:2). Christ called Satan "the prince of this world" (John 12:31; 14:30; 16:11).

According to the Word of God, the very air about us is filled with hostile forces attempting to destroy our fellowship with God the Father, and to deprive us of our usefulness in the Master's service.

But our Father God, in His great provision and plan of redemption, has given us a weapon to use against Satan. That weapon is given to us not only for ourselves, but also for the benefit of the Satan-ruled men and women around us. That weapon is the Name of Jesus!

Confession: *The weapons of my warfare are not carnal, but mighty through God to the pulling down of strongholds. Where Satan's forces have built strongholds, I can pull them down with the mighty Name of Jesus. Satan is no match for that Name. And that Name is a mighty weapon given to me to use against the forces of the enemy.*

BY INHERITANCE

God, who at sundry times and in divers manners spake in time past unto the fathers by the prophets, Hath in these last days spoken unto us by his Son, whom he hath appointed heir of all things, by whom also he made the worlds; Who being the brightness of his glory, and the express image of his person, and upholding all things by the word of his power, when he had by himself purged our sins, sat down on the right hand of the Majesty on high; Being made so much better than the angels, as he hath by inheritance obtained a more excellent name than they. — HEBREWS 1:1-4

We cannot measure the vastness of the power and authority in the Name of Jesus without realizing that He *inherited* that Name from God the Creator.

Jesus is the brightness of God's glory.

Jesus is the express image of God's Person — the very outshining of God the Father.

Jesus is the Heir of all things. And Jesus inherited His Name. The greatness of His Name is inherited from His Father. So the power of His Name can only be measured by the power of God.

And every believer has inherited the legal right to use the Name of Jesus!

Confession: *I know the Name of Jesus has within it the power and authority of the Creator! I know the power in the Name of Jesus can be measured only by the power of God. And I know I have a legal right to use that Name!*

BY CONQUEST

And having spoiled principalities and powers, he made a shew of them openly, triumphing over them in it.
— COLOSSIANS 2:15

This is a picture of Christ in combat with the hosts of darkness!

A marginal note in my *King James Version* reads, "He put off from Himself the principalities and the powers." It is evident that when the demon hosts thought they had Jesus within their power, they intended to overwhelm Him and hold Him in bondage. But when the cry came forth from the throne of God that Jesus had met the demands of Justice — that the sin problem had been settled, and man's redemption was a fact — then Jesus overthrew the hosts of demons and Satan himself.

I think Rotherham's translation of Hebrews 2:14 makes it even clearer: ". . . in order that through death He might paralyze him that held the dominion of death. That is the Adversary." Jesus paralyzed Satan! Jesus put him to naught!

There is authority in the Name of Jesus, because Jesus achieved the authority in His Name by conquest!

Confession: *Jesus Christ spoiled principalities and powers. He made an open show of them, triumphing over them in it. Jesus paralyzed Satan and all his cohorts. Therefore, there is authority in the Name of Jesus. And I have a legal right to use that triumphant Name against the forces of the enemy!*

RESURRECTION GREATNESS

*. . . He hath by inheritance obtained a more excellent name than
they. For unto which of the angels said he [God] at any time,
Thou art my Son, this day have I begotten thee? . . .*
— HEBREWS 1:4,5

*God hath fulfilled the same unto us their children, in that he
hath raised up Jesus again; as it is also written in the second
psalm, Thou art my Son, this day have I begotten thee.*
— ACTS 13:33

When did Jesus inherit His Name? When was
it conferred upon Him?

It was conferred when Jesus was made alive out
of spiritual death — when He was raised from the
dead.

It was at Jesus' resurrection that God said,
". . . Thou art my Son, this day have I begotten thee."
And it was after Jesus' resurrection that Jesus
revealed that all authority in heaven and in earth
had been given to Him.

Every statement regarding the fact that Jesus'
Name was inherited, or conferred upon Him,
shows that Jesus received the greatness of His
Name, the fullness of it, *after* His resurrection from
the dead.

Confession: *Jesus is Lord. He is risen from the dead, and He is
Lord. The power and authority demonstrated in the resurrection
abides in the Name He has given me.*

GOD-GIVEN

Wherefore God also hath highly exalted him, and given him a name which is above every name: That at the name of Jesus every knee should bow, of things in heaven, and things in earth, and things under the earth; And that every tongue should confess that Jesus Christ is Lord, to the glory of God the Father.
— PHILIPPIANS 2:9-11

This was done when Christ ascended on High, and God seated Christ at His own right hand, far above all principality and power, and might, and dominion. Another translation of Philippians 2:10 reads, "That at the name of Jesus every knee should bow, of beings in heaven, and beings in earth, and beings under the earth." (That refers to angels, men, and demons.)

Why was this Name conferred upon Jesus? Why was this Name invested with such authority and dominion? Was it done for Jesus' benefit? No. In the 2,000 years since Jesus' resurrection, ascension, and seating at the Father's right hand, Jesus Himself has not used that Name once. In fact the scriptures give no inkling that Jesus has *ever* used that Name! Jesus does not need to; He rules creation by His *Word*. But the Scriptures do reveal that the Name of Jesus has been given for the Church, the Body of Christ, to use!

Confession: *As a member of the Body of Christ, as a believer, I have a right to use the Name of Jesus — that Name that is above every Name!*

FOR HIS BODY, THE CHURCH

And what is the exceeding greatness of his power to us-ward who believe, according to the working of his mighty power, Which he wrought in Christ, when he raised him from the dead, and set him at his own right hand in the heavenly places, Far above all principality, and power, and might, and dominion, and every name that is named, not only in this world, but also in that which is to come: And hath put all things under his feet, and gave him to be the head over all things to the church, Which is his body, the fulness of him that filleth all in all.

— EPHESIANS 1:19-23

In every place where the Bible mentions the Name of Jesus, it also refers to His Body, the Church, because the Name was given to Jesus so that the Church might use it.

The ones who need to use His Name are those who have become joint-heirs with Jesus Christ; and those who are in contact with men and women in need of deliverance from Satan.

All that Jesus is by inheritance is in that Name! All Jesus has done through conquest is in that Name! And that Name belongs to the Body of Christ: It belongs to you and me! God has made this investment for the Church. The Church has a right to draw upon this deposit for her every need! That Name has within it the fulness of the Godhead.

Confession: *I have a right to use the Name of Jesus against the enemy. I have a right to use that Name in prayer. I have a right to use that Name in praise and worship.*

ALL THINGS

. . . For all things are yours . . . And ye are Christ's; and Christ is God's. — 1 CORINTHIANS 3:21,23

Most people wouldn't think the Corinthians could get anything from God; they were so carnal. Paul began this chapter by telling them they were carnal, yet he added, ". . . all things are yours."

When you were born into the family of God, the right and privilege to use the Name of Jesus became yours. Everything Jesus bought and paid for automatically became yours. But it is up to you to use what belongs to you.

Consider the story of the prodigal son. If the prodigal is a type of the sinner or backslider, and the father is a type of God, then the elder brother is a type of the Christian who has not strayed. When the elder brother came in from the field, he heard music and dancing. A servant told him, "Your brother came home, and your father has killed the fatted calf." The elder brother became angry, and wouldn't go in and join the festivities. So his father went outside and entreated him. "No, I'm not coming in." he said, "I've served you faithfully all these years. I never went away. I didn't go off and spend your money — and you never made a feast for me." "Son," the father said, ". . . all that I have is thine" (Luke 15:31)

Does God have what you need? If He does than it is already yours. But you'll have to appropriate it.

Confession: *All things are mine. I am Christ's and Christ is God's. The Name of Jesus belongs to me. I can use it. I will use it. All the Father has is mine!*

IN PRAYER

And in that day ye shall ask me nothing. Verily, verily, I say unto you, Whatsoever ye shall ask the Father in my name, he will give it you. Hitherto have ye asked nothing in my name: ask, and ye shall receive, that your joy may be full. — JOHN 16:23,24

This charter prayer promise is perhaps the most staggering statement that ever fell from the lips of the Man of Galilee.

What does Jesus mean "in that day"? Looking toward the future, Jesus was in effect saying, "I'm going away. I'm going to Calvary. I'm going to die. But I'm going to be raised from the dead. And I'm going to ascend on High. I'm going to sit down on the right hand of the Father. And a new day is coming. A New Covenant, or New Testament, is coming into being! And in that day, ye shall ask me nothing." This day in which we live is that new day!

"Hitherto [up to now] *have ye asked nothing in my name . . . ."* The disciples did not pray in the Name of Jesus while Jesus was on the earth. It wouldn't have worked. And they didn't need to, because while Jesus was with them, He met their every need. But the time was coming when Jesus would leave them. That was when they needed His Name. *The Name of Jesus takes the place of Jesus personally in performing miracles, delivering from Satan's authority, and bringing God on the scene!*

Confession: *I am a "New Covenant" Christian. I pray to my Father in the Name of Jesus. I ask in Jesus' Name. I receive — and my joy is full!*

DEMAND

Verily, verily, I say unto you, He that believeth on me, the works that I do shall he do also; and greater works than these shall he do; because I go unto my Father. And whatsoever ye shall ask in my name, that will I do, that the Father may be glorified in the Son. If ye shall ask any thing in my name, I will do it.

— JOHN 14:12-14

The verses in today's text have nothing whatsoever to do with prayer. In yesterday's devotion, we saw how Jesus said to use His Name in prayer to the Father. But here we see a different use of Jesus' Name. Here, the Greek word translated "ask" can also mean "demand."

An example of this use of the Name is seen at the Gate Beautiful. Peter said to a lame man sitting at the gate, *". . . In the name of Jesus Christ of Nazareth rise up and walk"* (Acts 3:6).

"Whatsoever you demand in my name I will do it." Let that soak in a little. Notice they did not pray. When we use the Name of Jesus, it is as though Jesus were here Himself. All the power and authority invested in Jesus, is in His Name!

You're not demanding anything of the Father. (After all, it wasn't God who had bound that lame man; it was the devil who had him bound.) No, you're demanding that the devil give way to the Name of Jesus!

Confession: *The Name of Jesus belongs to me. Whatever I demand in he Name of Jesus that is in line with God's Word, He will do it!*

DELEGATED

. . . Go ye into all the world, and preach the gospel to every creature . . . . And these signs shall follow them that believe; In my name shall they cast out devils; they shall speak with new tongues; They shall take up serpents; and if they drink any deadly thing, it shall not hurt them; they shall lay hands on the sick, and they shall recover. — MARK 16:15-18

Jesus delegated the power and authority in His Name to "them that believe." Some have relegated spiritual authority to preachers mightly used of God. But this passage of scripture isn't just talking about evangelists, pastors, or others in the ministry; it's talking about the entire Body of Christ — the *believing ones.*

Authority is invested in the Name of Jesus. And authority is invested in the Church of the Lord Jesus Christ upon the earth. Some of us have touched that authority now and then, but none of us have been able to abide in it like God wants.

However, I am thoroughly convinced that in these last days, just before Jesus comes, there will arise a body of believers who will learn how to take advantage of all that belongs to them in the Name of Jesus — that Name which is above every Name!

Confession: *I am a believing one. And these signs follow me. I will learn and know how to take advantage of that which belongs to me — the Name which is above every Name.*

KNOWLEDGE

*My son, if thou wilt receive my words, and hide my command-
ments with thee; . . . Then shalt thou understand the fear of the
Lord, and find the knowledge of God. For the Lord giveth wisdom: out of his mouth cometh knowledge . . . .*

— PROVERBS 2:5,6

Real faith is a child of the knowledge of the
Word of God. It takes no effort whatsoever on the
part of the intellect or the will of man to obtain
faith. *Faith accompanies knowledge.* As soon as the
light of knowledge comes, faith is there. As the
Psalmist of old said, *"The entrance of thy words
giveth light . . . "* (Ps. 119:130).

People often pray for *faith*. But what they actually need is *knowledge* of God's Word! When the
knowledge of God's Word comes to you, faith will
automatically be there. You could pray forever to
have faith, but if you don't get any knowledge on
God's Word, you will never get faith.

So, feed on God's Word. Meditate on God's
Word. Remember, *". . . faith cometh by hearing, and
hearing by the Word of God"* (Rom. 10:17).

Confession: *I will receive God's Word. I will hide it within me.
And I will find the knowledge of God, because out of the mouth
of the Lord comes knowledge. I will receive knowledge of God's
Word. And faith will accompany it. Faith comes by hearing, and
hearing by the Word of God.*

FAITH: AN ACT

But be ye doers of the word, and not hearers only . . . .
— JAMES 1:22

Some people have such a struggle. They say they are *trying to get faith, or else they are trying to believe.* But all that is necessary, is just to act on what God says.

I use the phrase "acting on God's Word" rather than "have faith" or "believe," because that's exactly what faith is!

Someone once asked Raymond T. Richey, a man mightily used of God in a healing ministry in years gone by, "What is faith?"

Richey replied, *"Faith is just acting on God's Word."*

Smith Wigglesworth would say, *"Faith is an act."* *That's what faith is — acting on God's Word.*

Confession: *I am a doer of the Word. I gain knowledge of God's Word. I hear His Word. Then I act accordingly. I act on God's Word!*

REALITY

Thy word is true from the beginning . . . .

— PSALM 119:160

People often make a substitution for faith — they substitute *mental assent*, or *mental agreement*. They mentally agree that God's Word is true, and they call that *faith*. But mentally agreeing with the Word isn't faith. You can mentally agree that the Bible is true, but it won't become real to you until you *act* on what it says. *It's when you act on God's Word that it becomes a reality.*

For example, you can believe in the truth of the resurrection as a great doctrine (and in some circles that's all it is — a doctrine or a dogma), but it won't mean a thing in the world to you until you can say, "Jesus died *for me*! Jesus arose victorious over death, hell, and the grave — and He did that for me! Jesus arose victorious over Satan! Jesus conquered Satan for me! Therefore Satan has no dominion over me! I'm free!

The resurrection won't mean anything to your life until you can say these very words. Then the resurrection truth in the Word of God will become something more than a doctrine, more than just a dogma, more than just a creed, more than just a theory — *it will become a reality!*

Confession: *I am a doer of the Word. I act on what the Word says is mine. The Word is true. I know it's true. So I act like it's true, and the Word becomes a reality in my life.*

ACT LIKE IT

Sanctify them through thy truth: thy word is truth.
— JOHN 17:17

The crisis of life come to all of us. If you do not know how to *act* on God's Word when a crisis comes, you will be at a disadvantage.

No matter what the problem is, God's Word has something to say about it. God's Word has the answer. Find out what the Word says, and act like it's true!

When someone asks the question, "What in the world are we going to do now?" Just smile and answer, "We're going to act like the Bible is true!"

Many people mentally agree that the Bible is true, but that's not enough. You must act like the Bible is true! If you know God's Word is true, and you act like it is, then it will become real in your life. *You will bring God on the scene in your life!*

Confession: *God's Word is truth. I act like God's Word is true. I act like First John 4:4 is true. I act like Matthew 6:25-34 is true. I act like Hebrews 13:5,6 is true. I act like Philippians 4:19 is true. I act like Matthew 8:17 and First Peter 2:24 are true. I act like all the "in Him" Scriptures are true. I act like it, and they are a reality in my life!*

THE LORD AT WORK

. . . For the battle is the Lord'S . . . . — 1 SAMUEL 17:47

"Don't get into any trouble," my mother called after me as I went to face a family crisis. "So-and-so almost whipped Dub."

"I'm not going to have any trouble," I answered. "I'll never have any trouble. I'm going to put the Lord to work."

The wife of the man who had caused so much trouble, met me in the driveway. She began to rant and rave, and plain old Texas "cuss." I thought, *Dear Lord, here is this poor old soul, full of hate and selfishness, and she can't help being that way. She can't help having the nature of the devil in her, because she's a child of the devil.* I didn't say a word to her, but I said to the Lord in my heart, "Thank God, the Greater One was in me." And I *acted* like the Greater One was in me (1 John 4:4). And He *is* greater. He's greater than the devil who was in her!

She must have sensed the compassion rising up in me, because she suddenly looked up at me and sputtered to a stop. Then she took hold of my hand and fell on her knees, crying, "My God, put your hands on my head and pray for me. A poor old soul like me needs something. Oh my God, pray for me!"

I hadn't said a word. All I had done was to act like the Bible is true.

Confession: *The Greater One is in me. And I'm going to act like it!*

HIS BATTLE

. . . Be not afraid nor dismayed by reason of this great multitude; for the battle is not yours, but God's.
— 2 CHRONICLES 20:15

I believe the Greater One lives in us (1 John 4:4). I believe Jesus is greater than the devil. I know the Word of God says that. Therefore, I must act like it is true. That's when it becomes a reality, and that's when the Greater One goes to work for me.

If I go all to pieces and act like I'm trying to fight the battle, the Greater One is not fighting it. And then I'm not taking advantage of the Greater One and what He has done for me. So I don't try to figure out the situation. I just lie down and go to sleep, no matter what's going on.

During the years I pastored, almost every church the Lord sent me to, was a church that had trouble. One in particular — no one wanted to pastor. God dealt with me before they contacted me, so I took it. But I didn't have any trouble. I rolled that church and its problems over on the Greater One. I would say to the people, "I'm not going to bother about that." I meant I wasn't going to worry, even if the deacons had a fist fight in the church yard. I would have just let them fight, and afterwards I would have gone to them, prayed with them, and got them lined up so we could go on with God.

Confession: *I refuse to battle. The battle is not mine, but God's. He is the Greater One, and I have put Him to work in my behalf by knowing His Word and by acting like it is true.*

61

REST

For we which have believed do enter into rest . . . .

— HEBREWS 4:3

Through the years, I've had the greatest time putting the Lord to work for me — just letting Him do the work.

In the half century since I learned about faith and that the Bible says, ". . . *we which have believed do enter into rest . . .*" I have been in a state of rest. Grasp what this scripture says! It doesn't say that we have entered into a state of fearing and fretting, griping, and worrying, or fighting. No! It says we have entered into *rest*.

I haven't seen a battle in nearly fifty years. When someone asks me, "How goes the battle?" I always answer, "The victory is wonderful!" There isn't any battle. I'm in the victory. *Faith always has a good report!*

Confession: *I have believed. I am a believing one. Therefore, I have entered into rest. I am in a state of rest. I act like I am in a state of rest. I do not fear or fret. I do not worry. I do not gripe. I do not battle. The battle is the Lord's. The victory is mine. I am in the victory.*

CHRIST IN YOU

. . . Christ in you, the hope of glory. — COLOSSIANS 1:27

By the power of the Holy Spirit, Christ is dwelling in you.

Is He any less Christ in you than He was when He was on the earth?

No! He's the same Christ. He has all of His power! He has all of His ability! He has all of His glory! He has all of His miracle-working power! He has all of His enablements!

And Christ is in you! You just have to know how to turn Him loose.

Somebody said to Smith Wigglesworth, "You must be somebody big; somebody great."

"No," Wigglesworth replied, "I just remember that the Scripture says, 'Greater is He that is in me than he that is in the world.' I just know the Greater One is in me, and the Greater One does the works."

How do you turn Christ loose in you? How do you put the Greater One to work?

You do it by faith.

Confession: *Christ in me is the hope of glory. Christ is dwelling in me — with all His power, with all His ability, with all His glory. Christ has already defeated all the power of the enemy, and He lives in me. I turn Him loose. I act like He's there. I allow Him to work by my faith.*

CASTING

Casting all your care upon him; for he careth for you.
— 1 PETER 5:7

Casting the whole of your care [all your anxieties, all your worries, all your concerns, once and for all] on Him; for He cares for you affectionately, and cares about you watchfully.
— 1 PETER 5:7 *(Amplified)*

Some people seem to take comfort in thinking *God knows and He understands,* while they continue to hold on to their cares. And they never get free from those cares.

It's not enough to know that God understands and cares. If you want to be free from your cares, you must cast all of your cares, all of your concerns, all of your anxieties, and all of your worries upon the Lord, because He cares for you.

This isn't something you do every day. It's a once-for-all proposition that enables you to get rid of your cares — it puts them over into God's hands.

I've done that. God has my cares. He's figured it all out, and He's working it all out. And I'm shouting while He's doing it! God is doing the work, and I'm shouting.

Confession: *I cast the whole of my care — all my anxieties, all my worries, all my concerns, once and for all — on God.*

COMMITMENT

Commit thy way unto the Lord; trust also in him; and he shall bring it to pass. — PSALM 37:5

A marginal note in the *King James Version* reads, "Roll thy way upon the Lord." Cast. Commit. Roll. Just roll your cares, your burdens, your anxieties, your worries, upon God. Isn't that what the Word tells us to do?

But God won't take your cares away from you. Some people have asked me, "Please pray that the Lord will lighten this load I'm carrying." God won't do that. God tells *you* what to do about your burdens. And if *you* don't do something about them, nothing will be done.

"You" is the understood subject of today's text: *You* commit your way unto the Lord. *You* roll your way upon the Lord. *You* cast all your care upon Him.

Some people don't get an answer to their prayers because they're not praying in line with God's Word. They're not doing what God said to do about cares, anxieties, worries, and so forth. But it won't do any good to pray about your cares unless you do what God tells you to do about them.

You can do what God says to do!

Confession: *I commit my way unto the Lord. I roll my way upon the Lord. I trust in Him. And He shall bring it to pass!*

WORRY

. . . Take no thought for your life . . . . — MATTHEW 6:25

Shortly after I was born again, I promised God, "I'll never doubt anything I read in Your Word. And I will put your Word into practice."

Everything in the Word was a light and a blessing to me until I came to Matthew 6:25. I learned from a footnote that the Greek reads, "Do not be anxious about tomorrow." Cross references pointed out that God says, "Do not worry." But I was full of worry! Not only was I nearly dead with a heart condition; I was about to worry myself the rest of the way to the grave. "Lord," I said, "if I have to live without worry, I can't be a Christian!" Suddenly everything in the Word seemed dark and fuzzy; I couldn't get any more light from the Word. My conscience smote me, because I was not practicing the Word.

Finally at 6 p.m. on July 4, 1933, I committed all my cares to the Lord. I said, "Lord, forgive me for worrying, for being full of anxieties, for fretting, for being discouraged, for having the blues, for feeling sorry for myself. I know You will forgive me because You said You would if I'd confess it. From this day on, because You have now forgiven me, I promise You the longest day I live, I will never worry again."

Confession: *I do not worry about tomorrow. I have no worries, no cares. I've committed them to God. I never have the blues. I am never discouraged!*

I CAN

I can do all things through Christ which strengtheneth me.
— PHILIPPIANS 4:13

Many years have come and gone since I cast my cares upon the Lord, and although I will confess that I've been sorely tempted, I have not worried. I have not fretted. I have not had the blues. I have not been discouraged, no matter what. (Some people said I didn't have enough sense to worry. But, thank God, I had too much Bible sense to worry!)

Worry was the most difficult sin for me to give up. Worry is the greatest temptation you will ever face too. But you can resist it. And you must.

Your worst enemy is the flesh. The flesh and natural human reasonings would limit you to your own ability. You look at the circumstances, influences, problems, cares, tests, storms, and winds, and you say, "I can't."

The language of doubt, the flesh, the senses, and the devil is, "I can't. I don't have the ability, the opportunity, or the strength. I'm limited."

But the language of faith says, "I can do all things through Christ who strengthens me."

Confession: *I can! I can do all things through Christ who strengthens me.*

STRENGTHENED

. . . The Lord is the strength of my life; of whom shall I be afraid?
— PSALM 27:1

. . . Whosoever believeth on him shall not be ashamed.
— ROMANS 9:33

The language of faith says, "I can do all things in Christ." The Lord strengthens me. I cannot be conquered. I cannot be defeated. If a natural force comes against me, it can't defeat me, because there aren't enough natural forces in all the world that could conquer the Christ who dwells within me!

"Greater is He who is in me, than he who is in the world." I am fortified from within. I've learned how to put Christ to work for me and in me. I have, dwelling in me, the Spirit of Him who raised Jesus from the dead! I have God's wisdom, strength, and ability in *me*. I'm learning how to let that wisdom govern my intellect. I'm letting God speak through my lips. I'm daring to think God's thoughts after Him.

He is the strength of my life, whom shall I fear? God has made me greater than my enemies. God has enabled me to put my heel on the neck of weakness, fear, and inability. I stand and declare that whosoever believeth in Him shall not be put to shame. Therefore, I cannot be put to shame.

Confession: *Make up your own confession from today's scriptures and faith thoughts.*

SWINGING FREE

Finally, my brethren, be strong in the Lord, and in the power of
his might. — EPHESIANS 6:10

One day in 1932, two hundred sailors were holding onto ropes attached to the dirigible, the *USS Akron*, as they attempted to moor the giant airship to a steel mast in San Diego. Suddenly, however, the dirigible shot straight up into the air. Some of the men hung onto the lines and were swept up with the ship, soon falling to the ground. Several were killed. After all the rest had fallen, one man kept hanging on. He could be seen as the dirigible soared high in the sky. People were screaming and fainting. They knew this sailor couldn't hold on much longer, and any minute he might fall back to the earth and certain death.

But after an hour and forty-five minutes, when they were able to pull the dirigible back to its mooring, the sailor was still dangling from the airship. An ambulance was waiting to take him to the hospital, but he said he was all right. People asked him how he had held on. He told them he had found he had about four feet of rope, so, while holding on with one hand, he tied the rope around his waist with the other, and the rope held him. He had just been swinging free the whole time!

Many Christians are also trying to hold on and hold out, but instead they give out. Some even fall. But all we really need to do is to wrap ourselves in the promises of God and *swing* free like the sailor, enjoying the scenery!

Confession: *I am strong in the Lord and in the power of His might. I am swinging free in His strength and His power!*

By Faith

. . . The just shall live by faith. — ROMANS 1:17

The faith life is the most beautiful life in the world! It is the life God wants us to live, and the walk God wants us to walk (2 Cor. 5:7).

Let both your words and your actions agree. If you *talk* faith, you must *walk* faith — you must act faith. Your actions and your words must agree that you are a believer. It won't do any good to talk faith if you're not going to act faith. And if it were somehow possible to act faith without talking faith, that wouldn't do any good, either, because your words and your actions must agree.

Some people declare one minute, "I'm trusting God to meet my needs." Then, with the next breath, they say, "Well, it looks like I'm going to lose my car. I can't make the payments." One minute it sounds like they're talking faith, but in a few moments their actions prove otherwise.

Some even quote God's Word, saying, "I know the Lord said in Philippians 4:19, *'But my God shall supply all your need according to his riches in glory by Christ Jesus.'* And I'm trusting Him to meet our needs — but it looks like we'll have to have the phone taken out. We can't pay the bill." They mentally agreed to the truth of this scripture, but they didn't *act* as if it were so.

Start acting like God's Word is true.

Confession: *I live by faith — faith in the Word of the Living God. I act like His Word is true.*

KEEPING HIS WORD

. . . I am watching over my word to perform it.
— JEREMIAH 1:12 *(NASV)*

You may be certain that if you accept God's Word and act on it, He is watching over that Word to make it good in your life. All you need to do is to *act on the Word*. It is very important that you learn this simple little lesson. Acting on the Word is not struggling. It is not crying. It is not praying. It is simply acting on what God has spoken, and that brings results.

Several years ago, after I had spent hours struggling and praying about finances and healing for my family, I lay exhausted on the wide altar of a church. Once I was finally quiet, the Lord could speak to me.

"What are you doing?" He asked.

"I came out here to pray through," I said.

"What do you mean by 'pray through'?"

"I guess I was going to pray until I had some kind of feeling or a witness that these needs are met. I'm 365 miles from home. I thought I would know somehow when my children were healed and our financial needs were met."

"Isn't my Word sufficient for you? You are not acting like my Word is so," the Lord said. "In fact, you're acting as if it were not so. You're acting as though you think if you pray long enough and loud enough, you might eventually talk Me into the notion of not being a liar and of keeping My word."

Confession: *I believe God. And I act like I believe Him!*

71

LOVE BORN

. . . God is love.   — 1 JOHN 4:8

. . . The love of God is shed abroad in our hearts by the Holy Ghost . . . .   — ROMANS 5:5

When you were born again, God became your Father. God is a love God. You are a love child of a love God. You are born of God, and God is love; therefore, you are born of love. The nature of God is in you — and the nature of God is love.

In fact, you can't say that you don't have this divine love, because *everyone* in the family of God has it — or else they're not in the family! They may not be exercising it. They may be like the man with one talent who wrapped his talent in a napkin and buried it (Matt. 25:25), but the Bible says that the love of God has been shed abroad in our hearts by the Holy Spirit. That means the God-kind of love has been shed abroad in our heart, our spirit, our inner man.

Romans 5:5 is not talking about the baptism in the Holy Spirit. It's talking about the New Birth — when you are born of the Spirit of God. That's when the love of God came in. When you were born spiritually, you partook of God's life and nature.

Confession: *God is love. I am born of God; therefore, I am born of love. I am a love child of a love God. The love of God is shed abroad in my heart by the Holy Spirit. My nature is love. It is natural for me to walk in love.*

MATURING FRUIT

But the fruit of the Spirit is love . . . .
— GALATIANS 5:22

I am the vine, ye are the branches: He that abideth in me, and I in him, the same bringeth forth much fruit . . . .
— JOHN 15:5

Love is the fruit of the recreated human spirit, produced because of the life of Christ within.

Picture a fruit tree. Where does the fruit grow? Fruit grows on the branches. Jesus used the illustration of the tree. Who are the branches? We are.

How does natural fruit grow out on the branch? It receives nourishment from the trunk — the vine — of the tree. Life from the trunk flows out into the branches. It's the same in the spiritual realm. God is life. God is love. His life and love flow out to the believers — the branches.

Fruit grows. It doesn't come fully mature. The Bible says, *"But whoso keepeth his word, in him verily is the love of God perfected . . ."* (1 John 2:5). The word "perfected" means matured. John was talking about maturing in the fruit of love. (I don't think any of us have completely matured in it yet, but some of us are making progress.)

Confession: *The fruit of the spirit is love. Christ is the vine. I am the branch. I abide in Christ, and Christ abides in me. Therefore, I bring forth fruit. As I keep God's Word, I mature in the fruit of love. I am making progress.*

THE LOVE LAW

*A new commandment I give unto you, That ye love one another;
as I have loved you, that ye also love one another.*

— JOHN 13:34

God's family is a love family.

And the love law of the family of God is
". . . *That ye love one another; as I have loved you* . . . ."

How did God love us? Did He love us because
we deserve it? No. God loved us while we were yet
unlovely. God loved us while we were yet sinners!
(And think about this: If God loved us with so great
a love while we were yet sinners and unlovely —
when we were His *enemies* — do you think He loves
us any less now that we are His *children*? No, a
thousand times no!)

Love is the only commandment of the love
family. If you love another person, you won't steal
from him. If you love someone, you won't kill him.
You won't covet his house. You won't tell a lie about
him. Therefore, divine love is the fulfilling of the
law.

Since love is the law of the family of God, one
step out of love is a step into sin. If you've made
such a step, repent and get back into walking in
love. To fellowship with your Father, to walk with
God, to walk in God's realm, you must walk in
love — for God is love.

Confession: *I love others as Christ loved me. Love is the law I
am under. I walk in love. Therefore, I have fellowship with my
Father Who is love.*

KNOWN BY OUR LOVE

By this shall all men know that ye are my disciples, if ye have love one to another. — JOHN 13:35

How is the world going to know us?

By our love. By this divine love. By this God-kind of love. By this unselfish love. *"God so loved . . . He gave . . . ."*

Now, His love isn't natural human love. Natural human love is selfish. As a usual thing, even a mother's love is a natural human love. It's selfish: "That's *my* baby!"

But if we would learn to let the divine love of God which is shed abroad in our hearts dominate us, it would make a real difference in our lives. It would cure the ills in our homes. Natural human love can turn to hatred when it doesn't get its way. It will fight and fuss, claw and knock, "cuss" and be mean. Divine love, when it is reviled, reviles not again. The God-kind of love is not interested in *what I can get,* but in *what I can give.* Do you see how that can solve all the problems in your home?

As children of God, the nature of God is in us — and God's nature is love. So it is *natural* for love to be in our spirit, our heart. However, if we allow our outward man and our mind to dominate us, that love nature in our heart is kept prisoner. Let's release the love of God that is within us!

Confession: *The world will know me by my love. I will release the love nature within me!*

LOVE ATMOSPHERE

Beloved, let us love one another: for love is of God; and every one that loveth is born of God, and knoweth God. He that loveth not knoweth not God; for God is love . . . . If we love one another, God dwelleth in us, and his love is perfected in us.

— 1 JOHN 4:7,8,12

Husbands and wives need to let the love of God dominate them — and not just natural human love — because natural love is so shallow.

Christians have an advantage over other people. Not only can they love their spouse with natural affection, but they can add to it divine love which never seeks its own, but always seeks the other's welfare.

In more than sixty years of marriage, my wife and I have walked in love. I never consider myself or what I want; I consider what Oretha wants. I never want to be self-seeking; I always want to put her first. And Oretha reciprocates. We always try to outdo one another in love. And how blessed it is! Praise God! Our home is like Heaven on earth.

A troubled person who had visited us once said, "When I visit in your home, it's like Heaven. You can feel a *presence* there the minute you go into the house."

We create atmospheres in our homes.

Confession: *I will walk in divine love toward those I love. I will let the unselfish love of God pour through me to them, creating an atmosphere of love!*

THE BRETHREN

We know that we have passed from death unto life, because we love the brethren. He that loveth not his brother abideth in death. Whosoever hateth his brother is a murderer: and ye know that no murderer hath eternal life abiding in him.

—1 JOHN 3:14,15

A minister's wife came to me greatly disturbed. "Brother Hagin," she said, "I can't go to Heaven. I hate my mother-in-law!"

After letting her stew a little, I was able to help her. I asked her to look me straight in the eye and say, "I hate my mother-in-law." And I asked her to check up on the inside of her — in her spirit — as she was saying that.

She said, "I hate my mother-in-law." Then she exclaimed, "Why, something seems to be 'scratching' me on the inside!"

"Yes," I said, "That's the love of God in your born-again human spirit that loves everybody. The real you doesn't hate your mother-in-law. But you're letting the outward man dominate the situation."

"You're right," she said, "I don't really hate my mother-in-law." And she made the spiritual adjustment of allowing the man on the inside, where love lives, to dominate the outward man.

Confession: *I know that I have passed from death unto life because I love the brethren. And I allow that love to dominate my being. I walk in love toward everyone!*

AN EXPOSÉ ON LOVE

Love endures long and is patient and kind; love never is envious nor boils over with jealousy . . . .
— 1 CORINTHIANS 13:4 (*Amplified*)

What about this God-kind of love?

What are its characteristics?

They are given to us in First Corinthians 13. It is to be regretted that the translators of the *King James Version* translated the Greek word for divine love, *agape* as "charity." My favorite translation on this "exposé on love" is found in *The Amplified Bible.* I think every Christian should read the *Amplified* translation of First Corinthians 13 every few days, if not every day — and practice it!

Let's look at it, beginning with verse four:

"Love endures long and is patient and kind . . . ." Many people endure long — but they aren't very kind while they're doing it! They just suffer along with people and things because they have to. A wife will put up with a husband, but she's not too kind while she does it (and vice versa).

". . . Love never is envious nor boils over with jealousy . . . ." Natural human love is the kind of love that boils over with jealousy. The God-kind of love doesn't boil over with jealousy.

Confession: *I am a love person. Therefore, I endure long and I am patient and kind. I am never envious, nor do I boil over with jealousy.*

LOVE ARISES

*Love . . . Is not boastful or vainglorious, does not display itself
haughtily. It is not conceited — (arrogant and inflated with pride);
it is not rude (unmannerly), and does not act unbecomingly . . . .*
                                1 CORINTHIANS 13:4,5 *(Amplified)*

It's always flesh that is boastful, haughty, conceited, arrogant, inflated with pride, rude, and
unmannerly.

And by an act of your own will, you can decide
not to give in to these fleshly temptations. You can
decide rather to walk in love — to walk in the
Spirit.

The battle is there between your human spirit
and your flesh. But the Bible says, *". . . Walk in the
Spirit, and ye shall not fulfill the lust of the flesh"*
(Gal. 5:16).

Decide to allow your spirit to dominate. When
the temptation comes, stand still a moment and
begin to speak the Word of God. Begin to say, "I
am born of love. I will allow the love of God within
me to dominate. When the temptation comes,
stand still a moment and begin to speak the Word
of God. Begin to say, "I am born of love. I will
allow the love of God within me to dominate this
situation."

And the love of God will rise up big within you!

Confession: *I am a love person. Therefore, I am not boastful or
vainglorious. I do not display myself haughtily. I am not conceited — arrogant and inflated with pride. I am not rude. I am
not unmannerly. I do not act unbecomingly. I act in love.*

79

THE BEST WAY

. . . Love [God's love in us] does not insist on its own rights or its own way, for it is not self-seeking . . . .

1 CORINTHIANS 13:5 (*Amplified*)

Take time to let today's text sink into your heart.

Too many people would rather declare, "Well, I know what's mine, though. I've got my say-so, and I'm going to have it. I've got my rights, and I'm going to have them." And they insist on having their own way, no matter how much their actions may hurt someone else.

I was only 20 years old and unmarried when I pastored my second church, so I rented a room from a couple in the church. The man of the house knew the Bible, and he had a marvelous experience with God. But he was the type of person who said, "I've got my say-so, and I'm going to have it. I'm a member of that church just as much as anyone else, and I've got my say-so." He had his say-so all right, and so did some of the others, until they wrecked the church.

This text says that love does not insist on having its own rights. Start believing in God and believing in love. It's the best way — and it's your way!

Confession: *I believe in God. And I believe in love. I am a love person. I do not insist on my own rights. I do not insist on my own way. I am not self-seeking. I am a love person.*

LOVE GAUGE

. . . Love . . . Is not touchy or fretful or resentful; it takes no account of the evil done to it — [pays no attention to a suffered wrong].   1 CORINTHIANS 13:5 *(Amplified)*

Here is the love thermometer — the love gauge! It's very easy to find out whether or not you're walking in love. When you begin to take account of the evil done to you, you're not walking in love. As long as you walk in God and stay full of the Holy Spirit, you won't take account of the evil done to you.

Through the years when unjust things have happened to me, people have told me, "I wouldn't take that. I wouldn't put up with that — not me!" But I just kept my mouth shut and never said a word, smiled, and stayed happy. Why, I wouldn't take time to deny it if they claimed I'd killed my grandma! I'd just keep shouting, "Hallelujah! Praise God! Glory to God!"

I suggest you walk in love, too, toward those who treat you in an evil manner. If you walk in love regardless of suffered wrongs, you'll come out on top in the long run!

Some people will regard your attitude as a weakness, however. Even ministers have told me, "There must be a weakness in your character; you never take up for yourself." No, it's a strength! *Love never fails.*

I simply refuse to hold any resentment in my heart against anybody.

Confession: *I am a love person. Therefore, I am not touchy, fretful, or resentful. I have no resentment in my heart toward anybody.*

81

A SECOND LOOK

. . . Love . . . Is not touchy or fretful or resentful; it takes no account of the evil done to it [pays no attention to a suffered wrong]. —1 CORINTHIANS 13:5 *(Amplified)*

The subject of walking in the God-kind of love is so important — and so overlooked by Christians — that we're going to take some extra time examining it.

". . . Love . . . takes no account of the evil done to it . . . ." This has to be the God-kind of love, because we were enemies of God, and God didn't take account of the evil we had done to Him. He sent Jesus to redeem us. He loved us while we were yet sinners.

". . . Love . . . pays no attention to a suffered wrong . . . ." We might just as well admit it — there aren't too many people walking in God's love, even though they have it! No they're walking in natural human love, and they sure pay attention to a suffered wrong! They get huffy about it. A husband and wife, both Christians, will become angry and won't speak to each other for a week because of some wrong that one of them suffered.

Can't you see how it would straighten things out in the home, the church, and the nation for people to become children of God, get the love of God in them, and then live in the family of God as children of God?

Confession: *I am a love person. I am not touchy. I am not fretful. I am not resentful. I take no account of evil done to me. I pay no attention to a suffered wrong.*

LOVE CHARACTERISTICS

. . . [Love] does not rejoice at injustice and unrighteousness, but rejoices when right and truth prevail. Love bears up under anything and everything that comes, is ever ready to believe the best of every person . . . . — 1 CORINTHIANS 13:6,7 *(Amplified)*

"Love bears up under anything and everything that comes . . . ." If you have the God-kind of love within — and if you walk in the God-kind of love — you will make it every time!

". . . Love . . . is ever ready to believe the best of every person . . . ." Natural human love is ever ready to believe the *worst* about every person! I've traveled across this country for many years in the ministry, and it's amazing what you hear about this preacher and that preacher, this person and that person, this singer and that singer. I don't pay the least bit of attention to any of these stories. I don't believe a word of them. I believe the *best* of everyone.

Children ought to have the right to be brought up in this love atmosphere in the home. Then they'll go out in life's fight and win. But when you always see the worst in the children and always tell them, "You'll never amount to anything," they'll live up to what you say. But when you see the best in them and love them, it will bring out the best in them. They will grow up to amount to something.

Confession: *I am a love person. I do not rejoice at injustice and unrighteousness. I rejoice when right and truth prevail. I bear up under anything and everything that comes. I am ever ready to believe the best of every person.*

Unfailing Love

. . . [Love's] hopes are fadeless under all circumstances and it endures everything [without weakening]. Love never fails [never fades out or becomes obsolete or comes to an end] . . . .

1 CORINTHIANS 13:7,8 *(Amplified)*

If you walk in love, you will not fail — because love never fails!

We are interested in spiritual gifts (1 Cor. 12 and 14), and we ought to be. The Bible tells us that prophecies will fail, tongues will cease, and knowledge will vanish away. But thank God, love never fails.

Yes, I believe in prophecy and prophesying. I believe in speaking in tongues. Thank God for these gifts! But if you exercise these gifts outside of love, they become as sounding brass and tinkling cymbals.

Let's have prophecy. Let's have tongues. Let's have faith. Let's have knowledge. But let's have love with it. Let's put love first, because we are in the family of love, and we have become acquainted with our Heavenly Father, who is love.

We ought to want to learn and grow in love until we are made perfect in love. I haven't been made perfect in love yet, have you? But I'm going to keep working toward that goal!

Confession: *I am a love person. My hopes are fadeless under all circumstances. I endure everything without weakening. I never fail!*

FEAR NOT

But straightway Jesus spake unto them, saying, Be of good cheer; it is I; be not afraid. — MATTHEW 14:27

God never comes with a message of fear. You can start in the Old Testament and trace all the way down through the New, and you will see that every time God manifested Himself to people, or sent angels or Jesus Himself, they always came with the message, "Be not afraid! Fear not!"

Fear doesn't come from God. It comes from the devil. And Christians, including preachers and teachers, have no business going around putting fear into people.

We hear so much fear preached: Fear of sickness and disease; fear of what's going to happen in the world; and fear of the devil. The way some people preach about demons causes people to be afraid. I preach about the devil and demons, too, but I preach that we've got authority over them. I preach that we should always remember, in all our encounters with the devil, that he's a defeated foe.

Fear is not the message of the Church. Faith is the message of the Church. Good cheer is the message of the Church. "Be not afraid" is the message of the Church.

Confession: *I am of good cheer. I am not afraid. I fear not. That is the message of God my Father to my heart. It is also His message to others. Therefore, my message to others is: Faith and good cheer. Be not afraid. Fear not!*

RESISTING FEAR

For God hath not given us the spirit of fear; but of power, and of love, and of a sound mind. — 2 TIMOTHY 1:7

Today's text calls fear a spirit, and it states definitely that the spirit of fear does not come from God. Today's faith thought is a confession you can use to successfully resist fear when it attempts to come upon you.

Fear,
I resist you,
in the Name of the Lord Jesus Christ.

In His mighty Name,
I resist you.
I refuse to fear;
I refuse to be afraid.

It is written in His Holy Word
that He hath not given me
the spirit of fear;
But of power,
and of love,
and of a sound mind.

I no longer have the spirit of fear.
I have the spirit of love.
I have the spirit of power.
I have the spirit of a sound mind.

DON'T TALK FEAR

Thou art snared with the words of thy mouth, thou art taken with the words of thy mouth. — PROVERBS 6:2

With your mouth, you are either going to give God or Satan dominion over you.

When you were born again, you confessed the lordship of Jesus Christ (Rom. 10:9,10). You confessed Jesus as your Lord. Jesus began to have dominion over you and to rule in your life. But, when you confess Satan's ability to hinder you, to keep you from success, to cause you to fear — even though you are a Christian — you are giving Satan dominion over you. And, naturally, when Satan has dominion over you, you are filled with weakness and fear.

Don't ever confess your fears.

"But what if I'm afraid?" you might ask.

"You" are not really afraid. The Bible says that God has not given you — the real "you" — the spirit of fear, but the spirit of power, of love, and of a sound mind. Fear isn't something that is coming from the inside of you, trying to get hold of you. Fear is from the enemy. *You* have a spirit of power — so say you have! *You* have a spirit of love — so say you have. *You* have a spirit of a sound mind — so say you have. When you confess it, then it will begin to dominate you.

Confession: *I am never afraid. I do not know fear. I have a spirit of power. I have a spirit of love. I have a sound mind.*

Godliness Is Profitable

For bodily exercise profiteth little: but godliness is profitable unto all things, having promise of the life that now is, and of that which is to come. — 1 TIMOTHY 4:8

Some people would have you believe that godliness — living for God, being born again, walking in fellowship with the Lord — has no profit in this life. They think we must simply endure life with all its ups and downs, struggles and trials, always bearing in mind that "this life will soon be o'er."

I'm glad Paul gave us a balanced viewpoint by saying that godliness is not only profitable "over yonder" in the next life, but it has promise of "*. . . the life that now is . . . .*"

As sinners, we were bankrupt, but God had mercy on us, and He sent Jesus to redeem us. Jesus came not only to save us from our sins — but to live within us (Col. 1:27). And Jesus wants us to bring as much glory to His Name, and to pay as rich dividends to Him as possible in this life. Instead of saying that godliness is a hindrance to success, the Apostle Paul says the exact opposite in our text scripture.

It doesn't *cost* to serve God — it *pays!*

Confession: *I live a godly life. I am born again. I live for God. I walk in fellowship with the Lord. This is profitable for me — here on earth in the life that now is, and also in the life which is to come!*

IS YOUR PROFIT SHOWING?

Meditate upon these things; give thyself wholly to them; that thy profiting may appear to all. — 1 TIMOTHY 4:15

If your profiting is to appear to all, then it is to show! Why is godliness profitable? Why is living for God, being God's child, walking in fellowship with God, keeping God's commandments, profitable?

It is because God has made some promises to His faithful children. Notice the word "promise" in yesterday's text: *". . . having promise of the life that now is . . ."* (1 Tim. 4:8). God had made us promises in this life. Our profiting is because of these promises.

And when our profiting (which is due to God's promises) appears to all, we are able to show the world there is a God in the Church — just as when Israel was walking with God, she could show the earth "there is a God in Israel" (1 Sam. 17:46).

Confession: I *will mediate upon God's promises and give myself wholly to them, that my profiting may appear to all.*

PROMISE OF PROTECTION

Read Psalm 91.

Paul said, in writing to the Church *". . . ye are God's husbandry* [garden, farm], *ye are God's building"* (1 Cor. 3:9). That means we belong to God. Now, if you have a building worth anything, even your own home, you are going to protect it every way you possibly can. And God, in His Holy Word, has promised us protection. I think the greatest such promise is Psalm 91.

Many years ago, I read this Psalm from a Swedish translation. I found that verse 10 translated in the *King James Version* as *"There shall no evil befall thee . . . ,"* was translated in the Swedish version as, "There shall no accident overtake thee . . . ." I researched it and found that this meaning is, indeed, included in the original text, and claimed this protection.

Some years later, I did some checking and found that I had driven nearly two million miles preaching the Gospel without having a single accident! Understand, I'm not bragging on my driving; I'm bragging on the Word — Psalm 91.

Verse 10 continues, *". . . neither shall any plague come nigh thy dwelling."* I claimed that part of the verse as well as verse 11: *"For he shall give his angels charge over thee, to keep thee in all thy ways."*

God has made promises and provisions for us. If our faith is not in God's promises, we live way beneath our privileges.

Confession: *Make your personal confession of Psalm 91.*

PROMISE OF PROSPERITY

Blessed is the man that walketh not in the counsel of the ungodly, nor standeth in the way of sinners, nor sitteth in the seat of the scornful. But his delight is in the law of the Lord; and in his law doth he meditate day and night. And he shall be like a tree planted by the rivers of water, that bringeth forth his fruit in his season; his leaf also shall not wither; and whatsoever he doeth shall prosper. — PSALM 1:1-3

When God's Word has a part in your life, and when you live by the principles of the Word of God, then what the Bible promises will come to pass in your life. Whatever you do shall prosper!

One translation of the last portion of Joshua 1:8 reads, ". . . Thou shalt be able to deal wisely in the affairs of life."

The Bible says concerning King Uzziah, *". . . as long as he sought the Lord, God made him to prosper"* (2 Chron. 26:5). The Bible says of Joseph, *". . . that which he did, the Lord made it to prosper"* (Gen. 39:23).

Confession: *I walk in godliness. I do not walk in the counsel of the ungodly, nor stand in the way of sinners, nor sit in the seat of the scornful. But my delight is in the law of the Lord. In God's Word I meditate day and night. Therefore, I am like a tree planted by the rivers of water. I bring forth fruit. My leaf does not wither. Whatsoever I do shall prosper.*